WORLD WAR II

The Story Behind the War
that Divided the World

NICK HUNTER

**BLOOMSBURY
CHILDREN'S BOOKS**
LONDON OXFORD NEW YORK NEW DELHI SYDNEY

First published 2015 by
Bloomsbury Children's Books, an imprint of Bloomsbury Publishing Plc
50 Bedford Square, London, WC1B 3DP

www.bloomsbury.com

BLOOMSBURY and the Diana logo are registered trademarks
of Bloomsbury Publishing Plc

The National Archives logo device is a trademark of
The National Archives and is used under licence.

Text design by Nick Avery Design

ISBN: 978 1 5266 0558 0

A CIP catalogue for this book is available from the British Library.

This book is produced using paper that is made from wood grown in
managed, sustainable forests. It is natural, renewable and recyclable.
The logging and manufacturing processes conform to the environmental
regulations of the country of origin.

Printed and bound in India by Replika Press Pvt. Ltd.

1 3 5 7 9 10 8 6 4 2

CONTENTS

STORMING THE BEACHES

Under the cover of darkness, a vast fleet of ships crept unseen across the English Channel. When dawn broke on 6 June 1944, otherwise known as D-Day, the ships' guns started a ferocious bombardment of the German defences on the Normandy coast.

As the shells exploded around them, the Germans would have seen the landing craft wallowing in the rough sea. These landing craft carried 133,000 troops from Great Britain, the United States, Canada and many other nations. Their assault would begin the invasion of France and, as they hoped, the eventual defeat of Nazi Germany.

▲ American troops launch themselves against the German defences on D-Day.

The invasion of the Normandy coast had been planned over many months by the leaders and generals of the Allies, which included the United States, Great Britain and Canada. They had hoped to leave nothing to chance, but the invasion had already been delayed by one day because of bad weather. Germany's leader Adolf Hitler believed that his armed forces, which had controlled most of Western Europe since 1940, would repel the invaders. Defeat for either side would mean disaster.

◄ Beyond the Normandy beaches, these paratroops are preparing to be dropped behind enemy lines.

Total war

D-Day was one of the most important days of a conflict that caused more death and destruction than any war in history. World War II's battles and bombing raids raged across Western Europe, Russia, North Africa, Southeast Asia and the world's oceans. By the time of the war's terrible end in the Japanese cities of Hiroshima and Nagasaki, as many as 60 million people had lost their lives. This book uses original and sometimes declassified top-secret documents from The National Archives to tell the story of the heroes and horrors of a war like no other.

WWII FACTS

D-DAY DIARY

Official war diaries give detailed accounts of the day-to-day experiences of units of the British army. This diary tells a small part of the story of D-Day. It describes the heroism of Lieutenant Colonel Dawson. After fighting their way from the coast, this unit "silenced" an enemy machine gun and mortar position.

WAR DIARY or INTELLIGENCE SUMMARY
(Delete heading not required).

Unit........4 Commando.
Commanding Officer ....Lt.Col...

Summary of Events and Information

▲ Plans for D-Day included artificial Mulberry harbours that would be towed into position as bases for unloading tanks and supplies for the invasion force.

HITLER AND THE NAZIS

The spark for World War II lay in the ashes of the previous war, stirred up by a man who claimed he could restore Germany's power. Germany had been blamed for starting World War I in the Treaty of Versailles. The Treaty was a peace settlement dictated by the victors of World War I. Germany had been stripped of territory, forced to dismantle much of her armed forces, and ordered to pay for the cost of the war.

Adolf Hitler fought and was injured in the German army during World War I. However, by 1921 Hitler's extreme views and forceful personality had helped to win him the leadership of the National Socialist German Workers' Party, also called the Nazis.

▶ *Hitler's extreme views were set out in his book* Mein Kampf, *meaning* My Struggle, *first published in 1925.*

Hitler's rise to power

Germany had been thrown into economic turmoil by World War I and unemployment soared when an economic crisis hit the world in

▶ *Hitler and the Nazis believed in ruling by force. Once Hitler was in power, he put an end to democratic elections, so the German people could not elect another leader.*

"I am told... that really the most dangerous man of all is the Führer himself. He falls into fits of passion and will listen to no advice... No one wants war; certainly, but when you have a passionate lunatic at the top who still commands the devotion of the populace and who is evidently prepared to run great risks, then already the situation is dangerous."

A secret report to the British government, by businessman Mr Law, who worked in Germany, written in 1937.

1929. The German people looked for someone to blame, and Hitler convinced many that Jews and communists were responsible for Germany's problems. In 1932, the Nazis became the largest party in the German parliament. In January 1933, Hitler became Chancellor of Germany. He ruthlessly attacked all opposition and in August 1934 declared himself Führer, the undisputed leader of Germany.

Nazi beliefs

Hitler preached that the strong German race had been betrayed by others, especially Jews and communists. Hitler's vision of a strong Germany depended on defeating these enemies.

▲ Jews were persecuted by the Nazi regime. They were also forced to wear the Star of David.

THE GATHERING STORM

Hitler preached that only military force could restore Germany's position in the world, lost after World War I came to an end. Many Germans believed that their country had not been defeated in the previous war. Instead, they believed that her military leaders had been "stabbed in the back" by the civilians who had agreed to end the fighting. Hitler immediately started rebuilding the country's military might, which had been forbidden in the Treaty of Versailles.

▲ *Veteran British politician, Winston Churchill, was sometimes the only voice warning about Hitler's plans. This telegram, which tells him about the invasion of Poland, shows he had been right all along.*

▲ *When war broke out, people were not surprised. Millions of gas masks had been distributed in September 1938 in case of an enemy gas attack.*

Turbulent times

The 1930s were a violent time in many parts of the world. In 1931, Japan invaded the Chinese region of Manchuria; Italy's dictator Mussolini launched an invasion of Abyssinia, East Africa in 1935; and Spain erupted in civil war between 1936 and 1939, which brought dictator Francisco Franco to power.

In March 1936, Hitler ordered German troops into the land west of the River Rhine, which, according to the Treaty, was supposed to remain free of German troops. Great Britain and France, desperate to avoid another war, did nothing. Hitler then invaded German-speaking Austria on 14 March 1938 and was welcomed by many Austrians.

German minorities also lived in Czechoslovakia and Poland. At the Munich conference in September 1938, Britain and France agreed that Hitler could take over the German-speaking part of Czechoslovakia. The Czech government was not even invited to the conference. In March 1939, Hitler established German rule over most of Czechoslovakia, breaking the agreement made at Munich.

▶ Neville Chamberlain was British Prime Minister from 1937 until 1940.

46

We, the German Führer and Chancellor and the British Prime Minister, have had a further meeting today and are agreed in recognising that the question of Anglo-German relations is of the first importance for the two countries and for Europe.

We regard the agreement signed last night and the Anglo-German Naval Agreement as symbolic of the desire of our two peoples never to go to war with one another again.

We are resolved that the method of consultation shall be the method adopted to deal with any other questions that may concern our two countries, and we are determined to continue our efforts to remove possible sources of difference and thus to contribute to assure the peace of Europe.

(Signed) A. HITLER.

(Signed) NEVILLE CHAMBERLAIN.

The last chance

Britain and France knew that they had been tricked at the Munich conference and now had no choice but to stop Hitler. The Führer, however, seemed determined on war, helped by an unlikely alliance with the communist Soviet Union. On 1 September 1939, German troops invaded Poland. The western allies protested, but Hitler did not back down. As a result, on 3 September 1939, Britain and France declared war on Germany.

WWII FACTS

THE MUNICH AGREEMENT

British Prime Minister Neville Chamberlain claimed that this agreement, made at the Munich Conference on 30 September 1938 would mean "peace for our time". Chamberlain's weakness convinced Hitler that he could take whatever he wanted.

▶ German troops invading Poland during September 1939.

BLITZKRIEG ACROSS EUROPE

Soon after Neville Chamberlain announced the outbreak of war on the radio, air raid sirens sounded in British cities. The government expected immediate attack from the air, but this was a false alarm. For most people in Western Europe, nothing much seemed to happen for the first eight months of the conflict, which was called the 'Phoney War'. In Poland things were very different.

Poland's pain

In their invasion of Poland in September 1939, the Nazis unleashed a new kind of assault – Blitzkrieg – meaning lightning war. Dive-bombing aircraft attacked, which knocked out much of the Polish defence. Towns and cities were bombed to create panic and terror. Tanks and infantry advanced quickly into this chaos. On 17 September, the Soviet Union invaded eastern Poland, as part of their treaty with Hitler. The Polish fought bravely but were forced to surrender on 27 September.

▲ *Around 340,000 British, French and Belgian troops were evacuated from the beaches of Dunkirk, leaving most of their equipment behind.*

War in the west

In April 1940, Hitler's armies marched into Denmark and Norway. On 10 May, the Nazi invasion in the west began. The Netherlands and Belgium were defeated in a few days. The French had built a huge system of fortifications called the Maginot Line to prevent German invasion.

▼ *British forces had been cut off by the German advance. They were forced to flee to the coast, where a fleet of large and small ships rescued them.*

German forces simply concentrated their attacks either side of the line, cutting off the French defenders. On 22 June, an agreement to end the fighting, called an armistice, was put in place, giving Germany control of northern and western France. A puppet government, forced to follow Hitler's orders, would rule from Vichy in the south of France.

With victory seemingly assured, Italy, led by Benito Mussolini, joined the war on Germany's side. Britain stood alone. Could it avoid the same fate as France?

▼ *Adolf Hitler visits Paris in triumph after the defeat of France.*

WWII FACTS

THE NEXT VICTIM?

The British Ministry of Information created this cartoon. The picture of Hitler preparing to attack left British people in no doubt about the danger they faced after the collapse of France.

BATTLE OF BRITAIN

Winston Churchill took over from Neville Chamberlain as British prime minister in May 1940. Churchill told Parliament that he had "nothing to offer but blood, toil, tears and sweat". Britain was in great danger. The defeat of France gave Hitler a base a few miles away from which he could launch an invasion.

Britain prepared to defend itself. Groups of Local Defence Volunteers, who were too old to join the armed forces or working in protected jobs, were formed. Lines of protection such as trenches and barbed wire were built to try and slow down the invading forces.

Battle in the air

But no invasion could be launched until the Royal Air Force (RAF) had been defeated. From August 1940, wave after wave of German fighter aircraft tried to defeat the Spitfires and Hurricanes of the Royal Air Force. Radar technology was used to warn the British pilots of German attacks. Pilots could be in the air within a few minutes. The German air force, known as the Luftwaffe, tried to bomb the airfields of southern England, but they failed to do enough damage to tip the balance in their favour. After a final effort on 15 September 1940, plans for invasion were cancelled. Britain was saved, for now.

▲ Winston Churchill's defiant speeches, radio broadcasts, and his refusal to consider defeat, inspired the British people through the darkest days of 1940.

▼ *The Royal Air Force lost 915 aircraft during the Battle of Britain, but factories produced 500 new aircraft every week.*

▼ *The 2940 aircrew who saved Britain in the summer of 1940 included pilots from Poland, New Zealand, Canada, France, Czechoslovakia, Australia and elsewhere.*

WWII FACTS

CASUALTY FIGURES

15 August 1940 was the start of the Battle of Britain. The Luftwaffe lost 75 aircraft compared to 32 for the Royal Air Force Fighter Command, as shown on this document marked "Most Secret". For the next month, German losses continued to be high, and their factories were not producing as many new aircraft as the British.

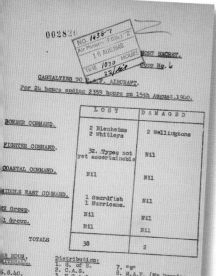

▲ *This report details how the British public felt about the war in August 1940. If people stopped supporting the war or the actions of the government this would weaken the war effort.*

BLITZ ON BRITAIN

After abandoning the invasion of Britain, Hitler and Luftwaffe chief Hermann Goering ordered huge fleets of bombers to bring the war into the heart of London and other cities. They hoped that these attacks would damage Britain's war economy and destroy the morale of its citizens. Thousands of tonnes of high explosives were dropped on London, especially the east end of the city, coastal towns such as Southampton, and industrial centres.

Black outs

Air attacks had been expected from the start. The cities were blacked out so there were no lights to guide the bombers. In the poorer districts families queued to sleep in the public shelters as the wail of air raid sirens went on around them. Others slept in corrugated iron Anderson shelters. People living in London sought shelter in the nearest underground station.

In the final few months of 1940, 23,000 civilians were killed and more than 30,000 seriously injured by the bombs. For the most part, the attacks strengthened the British people's resolve to defeat Hitler, but there were also examples of terror, panic, and the fear that invasion was still likely at any time.

▲ From 7 September 1940, London was attacked by German bombers on 57 nights in a row.

► This map shows how the German navigation signals made clear that hundreds of aircraft were heading for Coventry on 14 November 1940. Even if the British knew about the raid there was little they could do to stop it.

▼ Incendiary bombs were designed to start fires. On the night of 29 December 1940, as many as 1500 fires were started in a raid that was called the Second Great Fire of London.

◄ This map shows the bombs that fell on east London during one week in October 1940.

◄▲ St Paul's Cathedral in London surrounded by the smoke of the bombs and fires, and the scene after the smoke had cleared.

SECRET WAR

Intelligence and information were just as important as military strength in World War II. Secret agents were used to gather information about the enemy, but secret services also had double agents who deliberately fed false information from one side to the other.

The Abwehr was the German intelligence service. Many members of the Abwehr, including its leader Admiral Canaris, were secret opponents of Hitler. Hitler's Nazi Party also had their own security organizations, the SD and the Gestapo, which spent much of their time spying on the Abwehr.

Allied intelligence services included Britain's MI5, which was responsible for dealing with threats to Britain, and MI6 or the Secret Intelligence Service, which ran networks of spies overseas. From 1942, the Office of Strategic Services (OSS) did a similar job for the United States.

Double agents

MI5 was particularly successful at managing double agents. After the war, MI5 discovered that they had caught almost all of the 115 German agents working in Britain, and some of them were actually working for the Allies.

▲ Double agents knew the risks if they were caught. Johann Jebsen worked as a double agent for Britain. Shortly before D-Day he was captured, tortured and probably killed by the Nazis.

▲ *This poster warns Allied troops not to share military details that could help the enemy.*

▲ *This photo helped the public to identify German spies like the man on the left, who apparently wore worn clothing because of wartime shortages.*

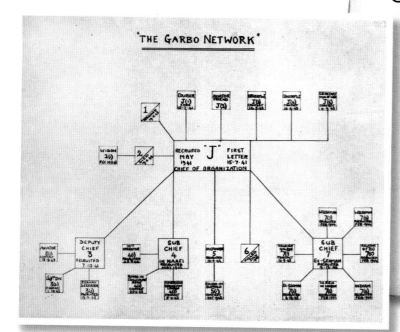

'THE GARBO NETWORK'

WWII FACTS

THE GARBO NETWORK

Spanish Juan Pujol-Garcia, codenamed Garbo, contacted German agents and offered to spy for them. He even convinced them that he was running a network of spies in Great Britain, when he was actually working for the British. Garbo's greatest achievement was to feed misinformation about the location of the D-Day landings. This helped ensure the success of the invasion and saved many lives.

CODEBREAKERS

In wartime, the element of surprise can be the key to victory. Knowing what the enemy will do next is almost priceless. Both sides knew the importance of keeping their communications secret, and breaking the complex codes used by the enemy was a major priority.

▲ An Enigma machine, captured by the British.

A German Enigma machine created coded messages and looked like a typewriter. An operator typed in a message and a system of wheels with letters on them would scramble it into a message that could only be read by someone who knew the settings of the code. Hundreds of mathematicians at Bletchley Park, Buckinghamshire, worked to keep up with the constantly changing codes. Alan Turing led a team to create an early computer, called the Bombe, which could decipher the code.

▲ Alan Turing.

Ultra secret

If the enemy ever discovered that their code had been deciphered, the advantage would be gone. High-level messages read in this way were codenamed Ultra and could only be viewed by the most senior and trusted people.

Hunting the U-boats

One of the greatest challenges for Bletchley Park was to crack coded messages sent to U-boat submarines that were attacking Allied ships. The Allies were able to capture several Enigma machines, which helped them to stay one step ahead of the German navy. However, successes like this could be short lived. For most of 1942, a new, more complex code had been developed by the enemy and could not be deciphered.

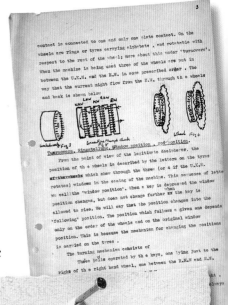

▲ This document forms part of Turing's explanation of the mathematical theory behind the Enigma code.

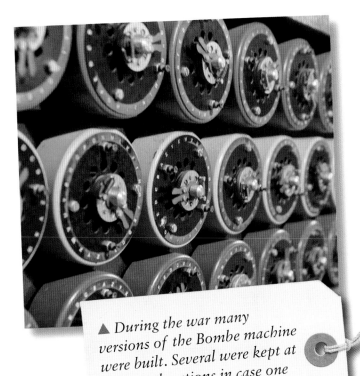

▲ During the war many versions of the Bombe machine were built. Several were kept at different locations in case one was destroyed by enemy attack.

CRACKING ENIGMA

Much of the work on cracking the Enigma code was done by Polish mathematicians before the war started. The Polish handed over their knowledge to British Intelligence just a few weeks before Poland was invaded.

▲ The Colossus electronic computer was built in 1943 to help with the unscrambling of German army codes.

OPERATION BARBAROSSA

In the early hours of 22 June 1941, Hitler took a huge gamble. He had invaded Yugoslavia and Greece in April. If he could invade the Soviet Union to seize oil for the German war machine, and food for the German people, Hitler would be invincible. Britain would have to make peace. The Nazis expected their plan would cause 30 million deaths from starvation.

▼ *German forces crossing the Soviet border in June 1941.*

Hitler's plan was a gamble because the Soviet Union could call on 14 million trained soldiers. However, these vast armies were unprepared for the invasion. After all, Soviet leader Stalin had signed a treaty with Hitler in 1939. The German forces quickly advanced deep into Soviet territory. The army was ordered to shoot all Communist Party members and Jews. The Soviet people destroyed cities and industry in the invaders' path so the German supplies would be stretched to the limit. But, by the beginning of October, German forces were close to the capital Moscow.

Siege of Leningrad

Leningrad (now called St Petersburg) was under siege for more than two years from September 1941. People starved or froze as all supplies had to come across a frozen lake. The people of Leningrad were reduced to eating crows or even carpenter's glue, scraped off the furniture they burned for heat. More people died in this one city than in the entire British and American war efforts.

▲ An officer of the Red Army urges his troops on against the invading forces.

WWII FACTS

UNLIKELY ALLIES

The war brought some unlikely allies together against a common enemy. Soviet leader Joseph Stalin stands alongside Adolf Hitler as one of history's cruellest leaders. His brutal dictatorship caused the deaths of many millions of his own people. However, without the Soviet Union's heroic struggle, Hitler may never have been defeated. In this poster, the British aristocrat Churchill and the communist dictator Stalin are shown as comrades.

The extreme cold of the winter, and desperate defence from the Soviet Union's Red Army stopped Hitler's advance in 1941. However, in 1942, the armies of Germany and her allies pushed south, hoping to capture the oil they had come for.

Comrades in Arms

JAPAN AND PEARL HARBOR

War in East Asia began several years before Hitler invaded Poland in 1939. Japan invaded the Chinese region of Manchuria in 1931 followed by an attack on the rest of China in 1937. In September 1940, Japan agreed a pact with Germany and Italy. Japanese forces then seized French and Dutch territories in Southeast Asia. As Japan flexed its muscles, protests from the United States and Britain grew louder.

▶ By the end of 1941, Britain had a new ally but also a new enemy in Japan.

Great Britain will pursue the WAR AGAINST JAPAN to the very end. WINSTON CHURCHILL

Surprise attack

Japan's leaders believed that a sudden, dramatic defeat would convince the United States to stay out of the conflict. They tested this theory on 7 December 1941, with a surprise attack on the US naval base at Pearl Harbor, Hawaii. In a few minutes, Japanese aircraft destroyed or badly damaged eight American battleships and killed 2403 people. American President Franklin Roosevelt had tried to stay out of the war but the Japanese attack gave him no choice but to join the Allies.

The British Empire still included many colonies in Asia, but they were now in grave danger from Japanese attack. In the weeks after Pearl Harbor, Japanese forces marched across Southeast Asia. Japanese tanks rolled into Singapore in February 1942. Burma was attacked so the Japanese could cut off supplies to China. The Japanese invasion of Asia and the islands of the Pacific moved so fast that Australia and New Zealand feared that they would be next. American forces were being readied for war, but it could all be too late.

▼ The battleship USS Arizona burns after being hit during the Japanese attack on Pearl Harbor.

▲ Japan's troops invading a Pacific island in 1942.

▲ President Roosevelt built a close relationship with Winston Churchill.

WWII FACTS

TIPPING THE BALANCE

This cartoon was produced by the British Ministry of Information. America's entry into the war meant a big shift in power, and a boost to morale in Britain. Could Hitler land a punch on the mighty USA, and its President Franklin Roosevelt?

WELL?

NORTH AFRICA AND THE MEDITERRANEAN

When Italy joined the war as an ally of Germany in June 1940, the conflict spread to another continent as Italian troops attacked the British in North Africa. The Italians were forced to retreat as British forces captured the Libyan city of Tobruk in January 1941. In response, Hitler sent one of his best generals to North Africa – Erwin Rommel, known as the 'Desert Fox'.

▲ *General Bernard Montgomery masterminded almost the first Allied victory of the war at El Alamein.*

Rommel's campaign of fast-moving tank warfare was well suited to the heat and dust of the desert. Despite having a larger force and better supply lines, British troops were regularly outsmarted by Rommel. Finally, in late 1942, the new Allied commander, General Bernard Montgomery, forced Rommel to fight in a tight space surrounded by ridges and minefields. The German tanks had little room to move and the Allies finally won a victory at the Battle of El Alamein.

Operation Torch

To the west, British and American troops landed on the coasts of Morocco in November 1942. Operation Torch enabled the Allies to encircle Rommel as he retreated. The war in North Africa ended in May 1943 with the capture of 250,000 troops from Germany and her allies, called the Axis powers.

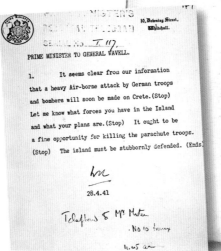

WWII FACTS

ADVANCE WARNING

This top secret message from Winston Churchill to General Wavell, his commander-in-chief in North Africa, was sent almost a month before German paratroopers invaded Crete. Cracking the German codes warned the Allies about the invasion. The Germans suffered heavy losses but were eventually able to seize the island.

Malta

The island of Malta was vital for both sides as a base for naval and air control of the Mediterranean Sea, and to disrupt supplies going to North Africa. The British-controlled island was besieged by Axis aircraft and naval power from 1940 until 1942, with defenders and ordinary people facing shortages of food and supplies. The Allies lost numerous ships trying to supply and defend Malta before the Allied victory in North Africa ended the siege.

▲ In desert warfare, there were no obstacles to hide behind. The armies used other methods such as this dummy artillery gun to fool the enemy.

▲ War artist Rowland Hilder's impression of the fierce battles fought over Malta.

▲ British and American troops land on the coast of Morocco during Operation Torch.

OCCUPATION AND RESISTANCE

As Allied and Axis forces battled in North Africa and the Soviet Union, much of Europe was under Nazi control. Lands on the border of Germany had become part of the German "fatherland", ruled directly from Berlin. The central area of Poland was named the General Government under Nazi rule. Nazi troops were occupying Denmark, Norway, the Netherlands, Belgium and much of France. In countries such as Italy, Hungary, Croatia and southern France, the governments were Hitler's allies or largely under his control.

Living under Nazi rule

People living in occupied Europe found life very tough, even if they were not part of groups such as Jews and Roma who were singled out for persecution. Everyone lived in constant fear that they would attract the attention of the feared SS, the Nazis' all-powerful state police who used torture and murder to achieve their aims. Food was scarce as Germany took a proportion of crops to feed its people and armies.

Resisting the invaders

Some people chose to work with the invaders, such as the Ukrainians who served as guards in the terrible concentration camps. Others bravely

WWII FACTS

SABOTAGE SECRETS

German agents carried some ingenious sabotage devices, such as this exploding chocolate bar. Although these were never used in Britain, several were seized in Turkey.

THE BOMB IS MADE OF STEEL WITH A THIN COVERING OF REAL CHOCOLATE. WHEN THE PIECE OF CHOCOLATE AT THE END IS BROKEN OFF THE CANVAS SHOWN IS PULLED, AND AFTER A DELAY OF SEVEN SECONDS THE BOMB EXPLODES.

STEEL ENDS

CANVAS

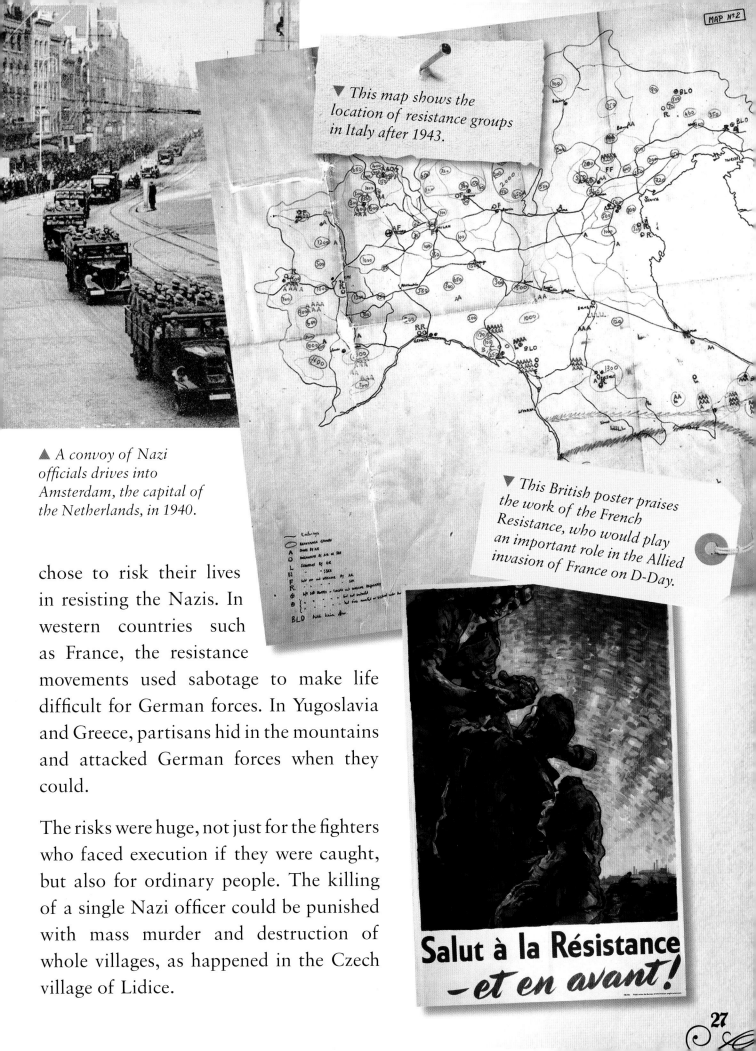

▼ *This map shows the location of resistance groups in Italy after 1943.*

▲ *A convoy of Nazi officials drives into Amsterdam, the capital of the Netherlands, in 1940.*

▼ *This British poster praises the work of the French Resistance, who would play an important role in the Allied invasion of France on D-Day.*

chose to risk their lives in resisting the Nazis. In western countries such as France, the resistance movements used sabotage to make life difficult for German forces. In Yugoslavia and Greece, partisans hid in the mountains and attacked German forces when they could.

The risks were huge, not just for the fighters who faced execution if they were caught, but also for ordinary people. The killing of a single Nazi officer could be punished with mass murder and destruction of whole villages, as happened in the Czech village of Lidice.

Salut à la Résistance
– et en avant!

BEHIND ENEMY LINES

The resistance movements in Nazi-occupied Europe were supported by the Special Operations Executive (SOE). Churchill set up the SOE to "set Europe ablaze". Agents were trained to work in secret behind enemy lines, helping the resistance and launching sabotage attacks. This secret unit began in 1940 based in two London flats but by 1945 13,000 people were working for the SOE.

The SOE's agents were trained in safe houses across Britain. They learned unarmed combat and how to survive without support after they parachuted into Nazi Europe. Scientists and camouflage experts worked on special equipment to help them survive and to damage the enemy, including exploding rats and tree trunk mould that could be used to hide radio equipment.

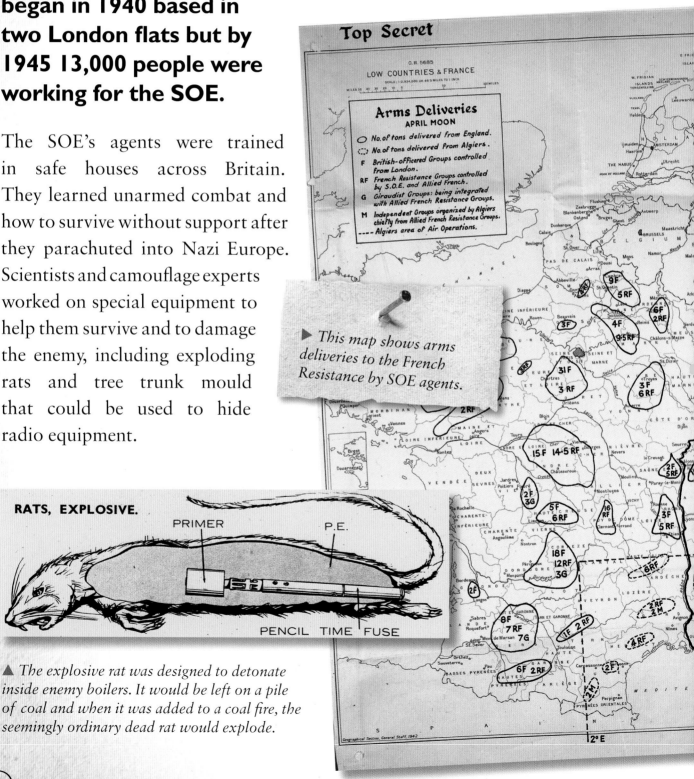

► *This map shows arms deliveries to the French Resistance by SOE agents.*

▲ *The explosive rat was designed to detonate inside enemy boilers. It would be left on a pile of coal and when it was added to a coal fire, the seemingly ordinary dead rat would explode.*

Sabotage successes

The SOE's greatest successes included blowing up a power station in France that stopped work on a German U-boat base. In 1945, the SOE destroyed a plant in Norway that was a vital part of Nazi plans to create an atomic bomb.

Other parts of British Intelligence were suspicious of the SOE. Some agents were believed to be double agents working for Germany. For example, the SOE radio sets in the Netherlands were discovered and used by the Germans to lure British agents into danger. Many agents were captured as they parachuted directly into the hands of the enemy.

▲ *SOE agents needed expertly forged documents from passports to luggage labels so they could avoid capture. SOE agents even created this false passport for Adolf Hitler as a joke to show off their skills.*

WWII FACTS

SPECIAL AGENT FIFI

The SOE had to be sure that their agents would not spill their secrets. The lives of other agents and resistance fighters could be at stake. 'Fifi' was a renowned agent who was used to befriend trainees. 'Fifi' was extremely beautiful and she would pretend to be a French journalist offering to help with the trainee's mission. If the student gave away too much information, they failed the test. Fifi's true identity remained a secret until 2014. Her real name was Marie Christine Chilver.

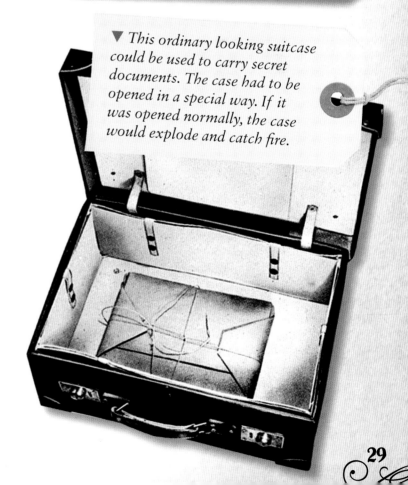

▼ *This ordinary looking suitcase could be used to carry secret documents. The case had to be opened in a special way. If it was opened normally, the case would explode and catch fire.*

THE WAR AT SEA

From the very start of the war, the Atlantic Ocean was a key battlefield. Britain relied on supplies of food and other materials coming from North America. Merchant ships travelled to Britain in convoys protected by warships, but they were still vulnerable to attack by German U-boats.

▲ *Saint Nazaire in France was one of the main U-boat bases. This aerial photo shows the reinforced concrete bunker that housed Germany's secret weapon. Saint Nazaire's port was badly damaged by a daring Allied commando raid in March 1942.*

WWII FACTS

RADAR

New technology had a vital part to play in defeating the U-boats. Radar detects unseen objects by sending out a blast of radio waves and seeing if they bounce back off an object, such as an aircraft or ship. Allied forces developed radar that could be carried by ships and aircraft. A German U-boat on the surface could be attacked and destroyed before its crew knew they had been detected.

During 1941 and 1942, German U-boats had great success against Allied shipping. Although aircraft could target submarines close to Europe and North America, there was an area in the mid-Atlantic where U-boats could hunt in safety. By 1943, the Allies were able to cover this gap. Growing German U-boat losses meant that convoys and United States troops for the invasion of Europe were able to move more freely.

Battles of the Pacific

Naval power was also crucial in the United States' battle against Japan. Fortunately, American aircraft carriers were undamaged by the attack on Pearl Harbour. These new weapons were vital in United States' victories at the Battles of the Coral Sea and Midway in 1942.

PLATE 12.

MERCHANT SHIPS SUNK BY U-BOAT IN THE ATLANTIC

WWII FACTS

COUNTING THE COST

These maps show the number of merchant ships sunk in the Battle of the Atlantic. They show that the German U-boats had most success in 1941 and 1942. In total, more than 2800 merchant ships were sunk and 40,000 sailors killed in the Battle of the Atlantic. Germany lost 781 U-boats. Being a submariner was possibly the most dangerous job in wartime as two-thirds of all U-boat crews were killed.

▲ *U-boat U-570 surrenders to a British warship. Captured submarines could contain valuable equipment and information for cracking enemy codes.*

◀ *Aircraft being prepared for launch from the deck of USS Enterprise during the Battle of Midway.*

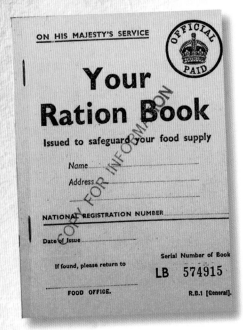

ON HIS MAJESTY'S SERVICE

OFFICIAL PAID

Your Ration Book

Issued to safeguard your food supply

Name.....................

Address...................

NATIONAL REGISTRATION NUMBER

Date of Issue...............

If found, please return to

Serial Number of Book

LB 574915

FOOD OFFICE.

R.B.1 [General].

▲ Shoppers became used to queuing in shops to get their ration books stamped.

HOME FRONTS

World War II was a 'total war', involving all the people, industry and resources of the warring countries. More civilians died in the conflict than soldiers on the battlefield. Even those people who were not caught up in the fighting or occupied by an invading army faced the regular danger of air attack. Every man, woman and child experienced changes to their lives, from the food they ate to the jobs they did.

Rationing

Essential foods such as sugar, meat and eggs were rationed in Britain from the beginning of 1940. German U-boat attacks in the Atlantic stopped many foods reaching the country. Rationing was designed to make sure that there was enough food for everyone. Other goods rationed included petrol, clothes and soap. Rationing of butter and margarine was introduced in Germany before the war even started. For most of the war, Germans did not go hungry, as the German government took food from the lands occupied by their troops.

War economy

In Britain and the United States, Government poster campaigns encouraged people to do whatever they could to support the war effort. 'Dig for Victory' was one slogan that called for every available piece of land to be used to grow food. In the United States, there was a great drive to collect and recycle metal so it could be used for war equipment. Many factories that had previously produced everyday goods switched to producing aircraft or other supplies for the war effort.

MAKE-DO AND MEND

says Mrs Sew-and-Sew

ISSUED BY THE BOARD OF TRADE

▲ Government posters urged people to mend their clothes rather than buy new ones.

Skin the cod, cut it into pieces about 3 inches long. Place in layers in a greased casserole, sprinkling each layer with paprika. Add the milk, put the lid on the casserole and cook in a moderate oven for 30 minutes. ...in the fish, keeping the liquid and making it up to ½ pint with milk or water. Keep the fish hot in the casserole while making the sauce. Blend the dry ingredients with a little of the fish liquid and made mustard. Boil the rest of the liquid and, when boiling, add it to the blended ingredients. Return to the pan and stir until it boils. Boil gently for 5 minutes. Stir in the vinegar and pour the sauce over the fish. Serve hot.

CHEESE SAUSAGE ROLLS

1 oz. fat
4 oz. flour
Pinch of salt

2 oz. grated cheese
Water to mix
½ lb. sausagemeat

Rub the fat into the flour and salt. Add the grated cheese and mix to a stiff dough with water. Roll out and cut into 8 oblongs, about 3" x 4". Roll the sausagemeat into 8 sausages, about 2½" long, and form into sausage rolls with the pastry. Bake in a hot oven for 25-30 minutes.

N.B. The fat may be omitted if the amount of cheese is increased from 2-4 ozs.

HOT POTATO SALAD

1½ lb. potatoes, sliced
1 small onion or leek, sliced
2-4 oz. bacon, diced
3 tablespoons vinegar
¼ level teaspoon mustard

1 level tablespoon sugar
½ pint water
Salt and pepper
2 tablespoons chopped parsley

Place all the ingredients, except parsley, in a pan and simmer until the potatoes are tender. Add the chopped parsley and serve.

RHUBARB JELLY

¾ pint of water
½ lb. prepared rhubarb
2 tablespoons sugar

1 tablespoon syrup
1½ tablespoons powdered gelatine
Cochineal colouring if necessary

Bring the water and the rhubarb to the boil. Boil gently for 10 minutes with the syrup and the sugar. Mix the gelatine with a little cold water. Remove the pan from the heat, and pour the hot liquid on to the gelatine. Stir until dissolved. Add cochineal if required. Turn into moulds and allow to set.

RHUBARB CRUMBLE

1 lb. rhubarb
2 tablespoons syrup
1½ oz. fat

4 oz. plain flour
Pinch of salt
3 tablespoons sugar

Wipe rhubarb and cut into small pieces. Simmer with the syrup until cooked and place at the bottom ... salt and sugar until like fine ... stewed fruit. Bake in a moderate...

Issued by the Ministry of Food

▼ A truck crosses a frozen lake delivering essential supplies to the besieged Soviet city of Leningrad.

▲ This calendar gave families ideas on how to cook nutritious meals with the rations they were allowed.

WWII FACTS

FAMINE IN INDIA

Food supplies were protected in Britain through strict rationing, but the story was very different in British-controlled India. Japan's invasion of Burma reduced supplies of rice to India, causing shortages and price rises. The government failed to act and the result was a terrible famine in 1942 that claimed more than 1.5 million lives.

The need is 'GROWING'..

DIG FOR VICTORY STILL

▲ The British people were urged to grow more food as imports were hit by the war.

WOMEN AT WAR

In the total war that erupted around the world, women were just as much a target for the bombing raids and other attacks as anybody else. They also played vital roles in winning the war. In the Soviet Union, women fought as fighter pilots, snipers and machine gunners. The British government introduced conscription for single women between the ages of 20 and 30 in December 1941. These conscripts did not fight on the frontline but worked to support the armed forces and did essential war work.

More than 250,000 women joined military organizations such as the Army Territorial Service (ATS) or the Women's Royal Naval Service (WRNS). As well as doing support duties such as cooking and administrative work, members of these services worked as mechanics, radar operators, drivers and delivery operators. In the United States, around 200,000 women joined the Army and Navy auxiliary services.

Women at work

Female workers took on many important jobs from men who were serving in the armed forces. One-third of British factory workers were women, making the aircraft, tanks and ships that would enable the Allies to win the war.

▼ It was essential for the railways to be kept running during the war.

WWII FACTS

WOMEN'S LAND ARMY

The Women's Land Army was set up in 1939 to help out on the farms that were so essential for the nation's food supply. By 1943, there were 80,000 'land girls'. Many land girls came from cities such as London and had very little training. They worked hard, in all weathers, and were not well paid.

'We could do with thousands more like you..'

JOIN THE
WOMEN'S LAND ARMY

▲ These members of the ATS are plotting the positions of ships. This had to be done by hand as there were no computer or video screens at the time.

◀ This poster makes women working in factories appear as war heroes.

WOMEN OF BRITAIN
COME INTO THE FACTORIES
ASK AT ANY EMPLOYMENT EXCHANGE FOR ADVICE AND FULL DETAILS

CHILDREN'S LIVES IN WARTIME

All children's lives changed during wartime. For some, the war meant separation from parents who were fighting overseas. Others were forced to leave their homes by enemy bombing raids. In Britain, hundreds of thousands of children were evacuated from the cities to the safety of the countryside. Millions of children across the world found their own lives in danger, or lost loved ones.

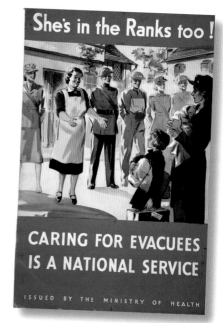

She's in the Ranks too !

CARING FOR EVACUEES IS A NATIONAL SERVICE

ISSUED BY THE MINISTRY OF HEALTH

▲ *This poster appealed to families outside the cities to take in evacuees. It points out that the children's parents were often in the armed forces or other war work.*

Evacuation

More than 1.5 million children and adults were evacuated from British cities when war broke out, although they often returned home when the promised air raids did not happen. Many came from the poorest areas of the cities and brought nothing with them but the clothes they were wearing. Other families made their own decision to go and stay with relatives in the country. Thousands of families chose not to evacuate their children, but quickly changed their minds when Britain was threatened by invasion and the Blitz in 1940.

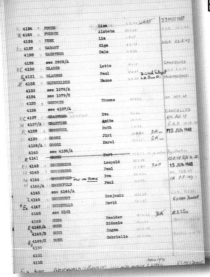

WWII FACTS

KINDERTRANSPORT

Many Jewish families were forced out of Germany by Nazi persecution during the 1930s. The Kindertransport was a British operation to rescue Jewish children from territories occupied by the Nazis. Nearly 10,000 children were rescued between 1938 and the outbreak of war in 1939. This document includes some of their names. The Kindertransport saved these children's lives, but many never saw their families again.

▼ Some children were evacuated to safe countries overseas. These children are on their way to New Zealand.

Children helped in the war effort too, especially the millions of young people who were members of youth groups such as the Boy Scouts and Girl Guides. Teenagers who stayed in the cities helped out as messengers and fire-watchers during the Blitz.

Children under attack

Most children in Germany were not evacuated during the war, and thousands were killed when the Allies bombed German cities. This was also the case when the United States bombed Japanese cities. Millions of families were made homeless by the fighting.

▲ Young people were happy to make their own contribution to the war effort. These children are helping to 'dig for victory' and grow food.

THE PROPAGANDA WAR

Adolf Hitler knew the importance of propaganda. When he became leader of Germany in 1933, he set up the Ministry of Public Enlightenment and Propaganda directed by Josef Goebbels. Its job was to promote the Nazi message of German strength and to spread hatred of the Nazis' enemies. The Nazis also made sure to ban all art, music, books or newspapers that did not promote their own view of the world.

▶ *Celebrating victories and the bravery of Allied forces helped to convince ordinary people that victory would come.*

Propaganda is any information or media that deliberately promotes only one point of view, usually that of a government. When war broke out, all governments used propaganda to raise the morale of their own people and attack the enemy.

British propaganda

The British Ministry of Information (MOI) had been planned even before the war started. It produced publicity aimed at British audiences on topics such as food rationing and reducing waste. The 'Careless Talk Costs Lives' campaign reminded people that enemy spies could be listening to their conversations. The MOI also made sure that newspapers and other media did not give away secrets or publish anti-war views.

Political warfare

Britain set up the Political Warfare Executive in 1941, which created materials that would damage enemy morale. They produced radio broadcasts in German to undermine Nazi propaganda messages. Leaflets were dropped behind enemy lines in an attempt to convince Germans to turn against their leaders.

German air raids and fear of invasion ensured that support for the war never wavered on the Allied side. Josef Goebbels wrote in his diary that, as the war wore on and there were more German defeats, Germans started to pay more attention to Allied leaflets and radio broadcasts.

▲ Letters to and from soldiers serving overseas were read and censored to make sure they contained no information that could help the enemy.

▼ This Allied propaganda poster was produced in Cairo, as part of the campaign in North Africa.

يوم الشعوب المتحدة

WWII FACTS

LORD HAW HAW

American-born William Joyce, known as Lord Haw Haw, broadcast Nazi propaganda from Germany to Britain. Living in Britain before the war, he had been a committed supporter of Nazi ideas. He was executed for treason after the war. Joyce's broadcasts supposedly contained details of which towns would be bombed by the Germans. Often these were just rumours intended to cause panic.

AXIS POWERS IN RETREAT

The Allies first real significant victory came in the North African heat in late 1942. At the same time, the Soviet Union began to turn the tide. The Soviet fight back began in the icy depths of the Russian winter at Stalingrad.

For the Soviet Union, Stalingrad was a battle of survival. If German forces could triumph here, they could capture the valuable oil fields and encircle Moscow. The battle-scarred Red Army fought for every building in the city, finally managing to put a stop to the German advance in November 1942. They encircled the attackers and on 1 February 1943, German commander General Paulus surrendered.

WWII FACTS

KURSK

The Battle of Kursk in the Soviet Union, in July 1943 was the largest land battle in history. Soviet and German forces included three million men, 13,000 tanks and 12,000 aircraft. In 12 days of fighting, the Soviet Union lost more than 300,000 men compared to German losses of 55,000. But the Soviet Union's Red Army could afford to take the losses, while Germany's resources were getting stretched.

▲ US troops crossing a temporary bridge in Italy as they try to force back Axis forces during 1944.

In 1940 Britain had been almost alone, but by 1943 the Axis Powers were heavily outnumbered by Allied forces.

Italian invasion

On 10 July 1943, Allied forces from North Africa invaded the Italian island of Sicily. By 17 August, German and Italian troops had been forced from the island. Allied forces landed on mainland Italy in September. Italy changed sides but the Allied campaign was not over, as their troops battled their way north against German forces.

In November, Roosevelt, Stalin and Churchill met at the Tehran conference. With Germany on the defensive at last, Churchill reluctantly agreed to an invasion of France in 1944.

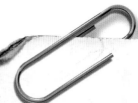

WWII FACTS

OPERATION MINCEMEAT

In 1943, the body of a British naval officer, William Martin, was found floating off the coast of Spain. He was carrying a top-secret document about Allied plans for an invasion of Greece. This information reached Nazi commanders via their spies in neutral Spain. The Nazis moved 90,000 troops to prepare for the invasion. But William Martin was actually a homeless man called Glyndwr Michael, who had died in London, and the real invasion was planned for Sicily. Operation Mincemeat was a trick dreamed up by British Intelligence to fool the enemy. The officer in charge of the operation wrote to Churchill saying, "Mincemeat swallowed rod, line and sinker."

GERMANY UNDER ATTACK

While Germany's armies were advancing across Europe, their bombing raids destroyed cities such as Coventry in Britain and Rotterdam in the Netherlands. However, after 1941, German cities were flattened by Allied 'area bombing', which was designed to hit the morale of the German people.

Air Marshal Arthur 'Bomber' Harris was in charge of RAF Bomber Command. Harris believed that bombing cities would win the war, even though Germany's leaders were much more worried about attacks on their factories and oil supplies. Huge bombing raids were launched against cities such as Hamburg and Berlin. British bombers usually attacked at night and the Americans attacked in daylight, supported by fighter aircraft.

▲ *Raids could include up to 1000 aircraft like this Lancaster bomber.*

WWII FACTS

DAMBUSTERS

Dr Barnes Wallis designed a special bouncing bomb that he believed could destroy German dams if it was released from the right height at the right distance from the dam. His plans are shown here. Wing Commander Guy Gibson and the pilots of RAF 617 Squadron were tasked with the daring Dambusters raid of 16 May 1943. The raid destroyed four dams and flooded Germany's industrial heartland.

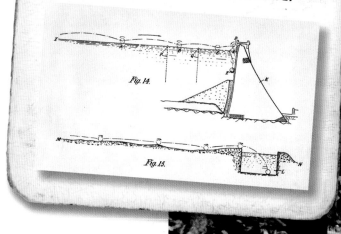

Fig. 14.

Fig. 15.

◀ *Arthur 'Bomber' Harris believed that the bombing of German cities would bring the war to an end more quickly.*

Justifying area bombing

Many people have questioned whether the death and destruction caused by these raids did help to win the war. After the destruction of Dresden in Germany just a few weeks from the end of the war, Churchill himself wrote, "I feel the need for more precise concentration on military objectives…rather than on mere acts of terror and wanton destruction, however impressive".

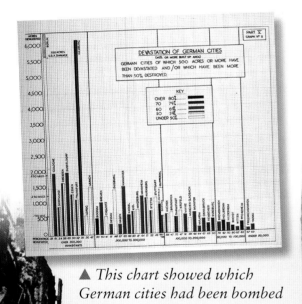

▲ *This chart showed which German cities had been bombed and how much damage the raids had done.*

WWII FACTS

THE HUMAN COST

In 1943, less than one in five bomber crews survived for a full tour of duty of 30 bombing missions. More than 160,000 Allied airmen lost their lives in the war. More than 500,000 German men, women and children perished in the raids.

This chart was produced to show what proportion of Allied bombing raids actually hit their

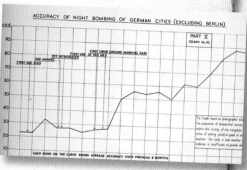

targets. Developments in radar and tracking technology made the raids more accurate. The low success rate of early bombing raids led to the attacks being targeted at whole cities rather than specific industrial and military targets.

◀ *This photo shows the destruction caused by an attack on the city of Hamburg in 1943.*

OPERATION OVERLORD

The first plan for Operation Overlord, the Allied invasion of France, was prepared in summer 1943. Working in utmost secrecy, Britain, the United States and the other Allies determined that the massive invasion force would land on the beaches of Normandy. If the invasion was to be successful, the Allies would have to plan every last detail, keeping their plans secret from the enemy. They would also need support from the resistance fighters within France.

WWII FACTS

OPERATION TITANIC

The night before D-Day, hundreds of dummy parachutists were dropped at various points in Normandy to confuse the defenders. This was known as 'Operation Titanic'. These cloth dummies were designed to catch fire on landing so it looked as if real paratroopers had burned their parachutes to stop them being found.

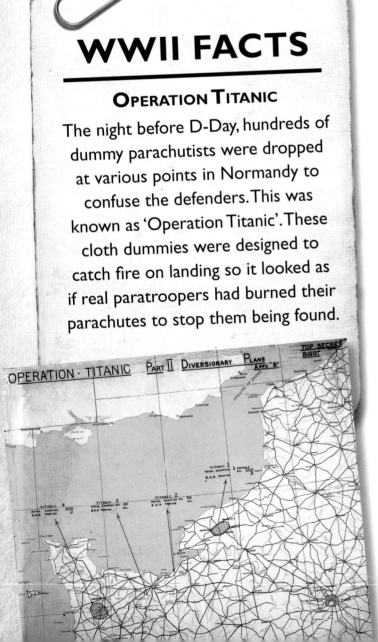

Decoy and deception

If the Germans had known where the invasion would take place, they could have concentrated their forces in one place but they could not be certain where or when the attack would come. Fake camps were built in south east England to convince them that the attack would be across the narrowest point of the English Channel, and in Scotland to pretend that Norway was the target. Double agent Garbo also fed false information to the enemy.

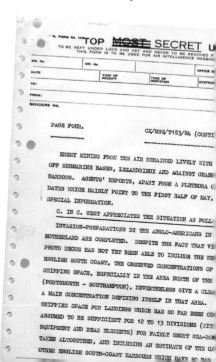

▶ *German coded messages told the Allies if their deception had worked and what the enemy knew about the invasion. This report from May 1944 confirms that the invasion force was almost ready but the Germans did not know when the invasion would come.*

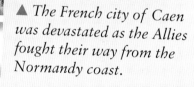

▲ *The French city of Caen was devastated as the Allies fought their way from the Normandy coast.*

Planning for success

The Normandy landings were planned meticulously. The Allies had even secretly collected samples of sand from the beaches to see whether the sand would bear the weight of their tanks. Even with these preparations in place, the German defences would still be formidable.

The D-Day landings were successful. US troops landing on Omaha Beach had to face the fiercest fighting and suffered around 3000 casualties. That was just the first step and it was several weeks before the Allies could battle their way out of Normandy. German counter-attacks eventually failed and, on 24 August 1944, Paris was liberated after four years of German occupation.

WWII FACTS

AIRBORNE INVASION

Thousands of Allied paratroopers were dropped into northern France a few hours before the seaborne invasion. Strong winds and anti-aircraft fire forced many of them off course, confusing the enemy about their real objectives.

45

TERROR AND PERSECUTION

Nazi rule in Germany and elsewhere had been built on hate and fear. This was especially true in Eastern Europe, where Hitler wanted to create extra 'living space' for the German people. He believed that terrorizing, persecuting and murdering the people who he conquered would help him to achieve this.

▲ *By the end of 1941, hundreds of thousands of Polish Jews had died of starvation and disease in ghettos.*

While the people of Western Europe had to suffer many injuries and crimes at the hands of the Nazis, the worst treatment was reserved for the people seen as inferior in the terrible Nazi worldview. These included Slavs from Eastern Europe, Roma people and, most of all, Jews.

From 1933 onwards, the Nazis built a network of concentration camps to imprison their political enemies. The camp system grew dramatically after the invasion of Poland in 1939. The Germans also set up labour camps where non-Germans were forced to work for the German war effort.

Ghettos

Some Jews and victims of race hatred were sent to these camps, while Jews from across occupied Europe were crammed into ghettos. These were areas of cities, often

▼ *German soldiers burn a village during their invasion of the Soviet Union.*

▲ *In Eastern Europe, both sides ignored international rules on the treatment of prisoners of war. Soviet prisoners were allowed to die of starvation and disease, and German prisoners captured by Stalin's forces were not treated any better.*

enclosed by barbed wire, where Jews were forced to live with very little food, sanitation or medical supplies. There were around 1000 such ghettos in Europe.

The ghettos were a way to separate Jews from the rest of the population while the Nazis decided their fate.

WWII FACTS

JAPANESE RULE

Japanese occupation of Southeast Asia could be just as brutal as the Nazi regime in Europe. In Singapore, the Chinese community was singled out for terrible treatment, including the murder of thousands of people. Around five million people died as a result of Japanese rule in Asia.

◀ *The Star of David on this concentration camp uniform shows that it was worn by a prisoner whose only crime was to be Jewish.*

The Nazis' 'Final Solution'

In July 1941, Reinhard Heydrich, a senior officer in the SS, was ordered to devise a "final solution to the Jewish question". His plan, which was approved at a conference in January 1942, was nothing less than the murder of 11 million Jews across Europe.

Jews across Europe were transported from their home countries to camps in Poland and Eastern Europe. Those who were physically strong would be put to work. Others would be murdered on an industrial scale. More than one million people were sent to the largest death camp at Auschwitz. Further east, Jewish ghettos were destroyed and the inhabitants killed. In total, around six million Jews died in the Holocaust.

▼ Allied codebreakers started picking up reports of widespread killing of Jews shortly after the invasion of the Soviet Union in 1941. This document from 1942 warns about the Nazi plans to murder all Jews in occupied Europe.

[CYPHER].

FROM BERNE TO FOREIGN OFFICE.

Mr. Norton.   D. 4.48 p.m. August 10th, 1942.
No. 2851.   R. 6.25 p.m. August 10th, 1942.
August 10th, 1942.

уууууу

Following from His Majesty's Consul General at Geneva No. 174 (Begins).

Following for Mr. S.S. Silverman M.P., Chairman of British Section, World Jewish Congress London from Mr. Gerhart Riegner Secretary of World Jewish Congress, Geneva.

[Begins].

Received alarming report stating that, in the Fuehrer's Headquarters, a plan has been discussed, and is under consideration according to which all Jews in countries occupied or controlled by Germany numbering 3½ to 4 millions should, after deportation and concentration in the East, be at one blow exterminated, in order to resolve, once and for all the Jewish question in Europe. Action is reported to be planned for the autumn. Ways of execution are still being discussed including the use of prussic acid. We transmit this information with all the necessary reservation, as exactitude cannot be confirmed by us. Our informant is reported to have close connexions with the highest German authorities, and his reports are generally reliable. Please inform and consult New York. (Ends).

▼ Survivors of Auschwitz concentration camp when it was finally liberated in January 1945.

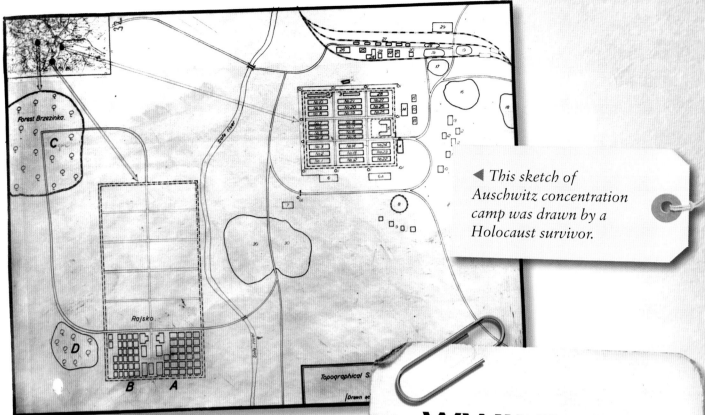

◀ *This sketch of Auschwitz concentration camp was drawn by a Holocaust survivor.*

Who knew about the Holocaust?

While the orders for the Holocaust came from the top of the Nazi Party and were kept as secret as possible, thousands of people were involved in the administration of this gigantic crime. Many of the brutal camp guards were not German but came from the occupied countries of Eastern Europe. The Nazis' victims were transported across Europe tightly packed in windowless trains. The officials who organized these forced journeys, or ran the factories employing Jewish slave labour, knew something of what was going on. While some people risked their own lives to protect Jews, many who knew the truth remained silent.

WWII FACTS

WHAT DID THE ALLIES KNOW?

This report from 1942 shows that the Allies had some knowledge of what was happening. Around four million Jews were executed in that year. At that time, Nazi power was at its height. The full horrors of camps such as Auschwitz and Belsen were not discovered until they were found in 1945, but could the Allies have done more to stop the Holocaust?

MOST SECRET

40/42. 2.

10. Reports on deaths in German prison camps during August reveal the following figures:-

NIEDERHAGEN: 21;   AUSCHWITZ: 6829 men, 1525 women;
FLOSSENBURG: 88;   BUCHENWALD: 74. (1/9).
A message of 4/9, in reply to a request for 1000 prisoners for building the DANUBE railway, states that AUSCHWITZ cannot provide them until the "ban" (Lagersperre) on the AUSCHWITZ camp has been lifted. It appears that although typhus is still rife at AUSCHWITZ, new arrivals continue to come in.

11. As from 1/9/42, "natural deaths" among prisoners in Concentration Camps are to be reported apparently only in writing (durch Formblatt).

Hitler's Downfall

By the close of 1944, the end of the war was in sight. Both Germany and Japan were exhausted and surrounded by their enemies. But their leaders were determined to fight on until their inevitable defeat. The Nazi leaders knew that their crimes, and the thirst for revenge of the Soviet Union, meant that they could never make peace.

In October 1944, the armies that had invaded France reached the River Rhine, in western Germany. Hitler's forces launched one last counter-attack into Belgium, but this soon fizzled out. In the East, the Soviet Union's Red Army marched on towards Berlin.

Germans and others fled ahead of the Soviet advance. They were desperate to reach the land controlled by the United States and British forces, who would treat the defeated Germans better than Stalin's vengeful army.

The two Allied armies met each other on 24 April, but the fighting continued in many areas including Hitler's capital Berlin. By the end of April, the Soviet army was fighting its way into Berlin and Hitler took his own life in his underground bunker in the city on 30 April.

▼ *The war left millions without homes or families, like this boy in the ruins of Warsaw, Poland.*

Victory in Europe

The final German surrender was agreed on 8 May 1945 and this was celebrated as Victory in Europe Day, or VE Day. There was excitement and relief in cities such as London and Paris. Hitler had promised to make Germany great again, but left behind a shattered country. Millions of Germans became refugees in their own country. Germans also had to face the horror of the death camps and the crimes that had been committed in their name.

▼ *German troops taken prisoner at Aachen on the German border in October 1944.*

▶ *This surrender of German forces was signed on 8 May 1945, ending the war in Europe.*

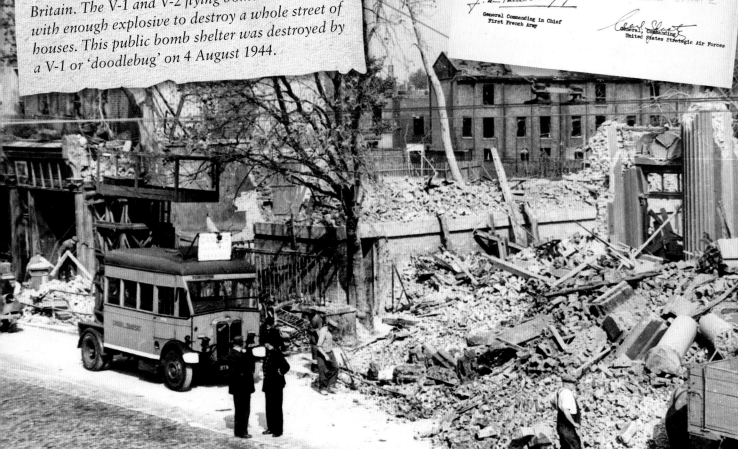

▼ *In 1944, Hitler unleashed a new menace on Britain. The V-1 and V-2 flying bombs were packed with enough explosive to destroy a whole street of houses. This public bomb shelter was destroyed by a V-1 or 'doodlebug' on 4 August 1944.*

WAR AND PEACE IN THE PACIFIC

Even after Hitler was defeated in Europe, Japan refused to surrender. The Pacific conflict was very different from the battles in Europe. Japanese forces were established in Southeast Asia and controlled many scattered islands of the Pacific. To get within striking distance of Japan, American forces had to capture these islands. One thing that the Japanese forces shared with the Nazis was their appalling treatment of their prisoners and the people who lived under their rule.

▲ *High school girls wave as a kamikaze pilot sets off on his final journey.*

Island assaults

Japanese soldiers fought fiercely to defend their island fortresses. Of the 30,000 men defending the island of Saipan, almost none survived the American assault as they refused to surrender. In 1944, the Americans got closer to Japan with the capture of the Marianas Islands and then the Philippines.

The might of American industry enabled them to build far more ships and aircraft than their enemy. By the end of 1944, American aircraft were close enough to launch bombing raids on Japanese cities. In February 1945, they captured the southern Japanese island of Iwo Jima. Japan's response grew even more desperate, as kamikaze pilots crashed their explosives-laden planes into American ships, killing many Americans and sacrificing their own lives.

▲ *By the time Churchill, Roosevelt and Stalin met at Yalta in February 1945 it was clear that the United States and the Soviet Union would dominate the world after the war.*

The final act

The United States then had to make a decision about whether to use a new and terrible weapon. Many thousands of American soldiers would be killed in invading Japan, and the war would last longer. President Harry Truman, who had taken office after the death of President Roosevelt, authorized the use of the first atomic bomb, developed over many years, on the city of Hiroshima.

Hiroshima was destroyed in a blinding flash of light and heat on 6 August 1945, killing 80,000 people. Another bomb was dropped on Nagasaki three days later, before Japan surrendered on 15 August. The most destructive, hate-filled conflict in history was finally over.

◄ *The atomic bomb explosion destroyed around half of the city of Nagasaki and claimed 30,000 lives.*

◄ *The bomb that exploded over Nagasaki had an explosive power equivalent to around 20,000 tonnes of TNT.*

Thirteen Japanese flying-boats were smashed in a heavy Royal Air Force raid on the harbour of Port Blair in the Andaman Islands.

SMASH JAPANESE AGGRESSION!

◄ *A British poster rallies support for the war against Japan. British, Indian and African troops battled the Japanese in the jungles of Burma until 1945.*

WWII FACTS

NO SURRENDER

One Japanese soldier continued the war for almost 30 years after the Japanese surrender. Lieutenant Hiroo Onoda carried on fighting on a remote Philippine island until March 1974. He refused to surrender until he received official orders from Japan.

WORLD WAR TO COLD WAR

As victory in World War II edged closer, it became clear that the post-war world would be very different. Two countries had emerged as global powers – the capitalist United States and the communist Soviet Union. Although these superpowers had fought together against Hitler, their political ideas were very different.

Cold War

Germany was divided between the area controlled by the Soviet Union, which became East Germany, and West Germany controlled by the United States and Britain. In East Germany, Stalin imposed a communist government, as he did in much of Soviet-controlled Eastern Europe. Western countries such as France might have been taken over by communists if the United States had not provided money for rebuilding. Under the Marshall Plan of 1947, the United States gave $17 billion to the devastated countries of Europe.

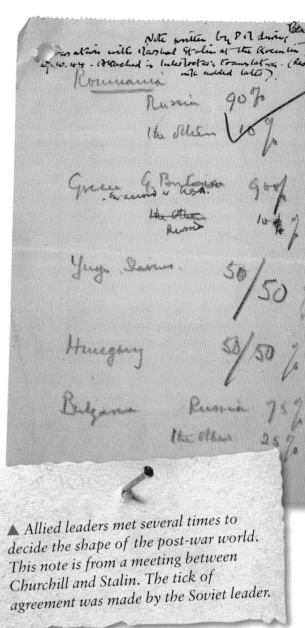

▲ *Allied leaders met several times to decide the shape of the post-war world. This note is from a meeting between Churchill and Stalin. The tick of agreement was made by the Soviet leader.*

▶ *In 1961, the communist authorities in East Berlin built a huge wall to stop people moving to the western part of the city. Here, US President Kennedy visits this symbol of the Cold War in 1963.*

The two superpowers, both with nuclear weapons after 1949, opposed each other in an uneasy mixture of peace and war until 1989, called the Cold War. The two parts of Germany were reunified in 1990.

While Britain had stood alone against the Nazis, the country was greatly weakened by the sacrifice of winning the war. In the Cold-War world, Britain's influence declined and most of the lands that had been part of its empire gained independence.

▼ *Surviving Nazi leaders on trial in 1945.*

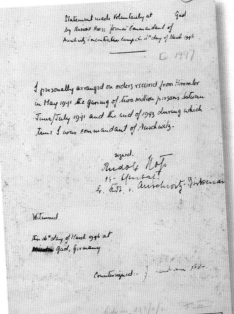

WWII FACTS

NAZIS ON TRIAL

From November 1945, leading Nazis were put on trial for their role in the regime's crimes, including crimes against humanity. There were a total of 13 trials held at Nuremberg between 1945 and 1949. Those on trial included leading Nazis such as Hermann Goering, Hitler's chosen successor. Other Nazis faced trial elsewhere, including Rudolph Hoess, commandant of Auschwitz concentration camp, who signed this confession to confirm that he had ordered the murder of two million people. Hoess was executed in 1947.

LOOKING FOR CLUES

There are many physical reminders of the war present today, such as buildings and memorials. These have been built or preserved to remind people about the terrible events that took place between 1939 and 1945.

▶ *There are millions of photographs and other sources that tell the story of the war. Many of them are preserved in The National Archives and included in this book. This photo shows a Red Cross worker writing a letter home for an injured soldier.*

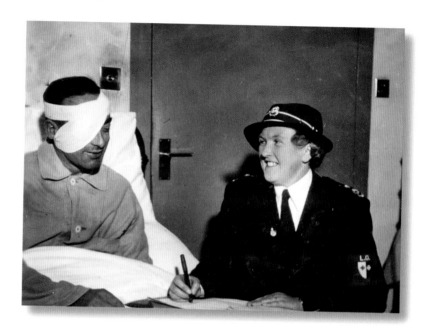

▼ *It can be hard to imagine the fierce battles fought on the peaceful beaches of Normandy. However, there are many reminders including gun emplacements, fortifications and memorials to those who died. In this picture, you can see the remains of one of the Mulberry harbours used in the invasion.*

▶ Beneath the streets of London, visitors can explore the underground bunker used by Winston Churchill and the British government during the darkest days of the war. The Map Room was constantly staffed throughout the war, mapping the progress of the Allied armies and navies around the world. This room is where Churchill met his ministers and generals while the bombs fell on London. The Churchill War Rooms are now a museum.

◀ This Memorial to the Murdered Jews of Europe stands in the centre of Berlin, Germany. It was opened in 1999, after Germany had been reunited. Its field of 2700 concrete slabs or 'stelae' are designed to represent the huge scale of the Holocaust. There are also memorials to other victims of the Nazis, such as the Roma people, homosexuals and the disabled.

▶ Auschwitz-Birkenau was the major centre for the murder of Jews and others during the war. Today, this death camp in Poland has been preserved as a World Heritage Site. According to UNESCO, part of the United Nations organization, the barbed wire, barracks and gas chambers of Auschwitz are a permanent symbol of "humanity's cruelty to its fellow human beings in the 20th Century".

WORLD WAR II TIMELINE

1939

23 August Nazi-Soviet Pact agreed between Hitler and Stalin, allowing Germany to invade Poland without being attacked by the Soviet Union.

1 September German troops invade Poland. Poland surrenders on 27 September.

3 September Britain and France declare war on Germany.

1940

9 April Germany begins invasion of Denmark and Norway.

10 May Germany invades Belgium and the Netherlands. German forces cross the French border on 12 May.

27 May Evacuation of 340,000 Allied soldiers from Dunkirk, France, begins.

10 June Italy joins the war as an ally of Germany.

22 June Armistice signed between Germany and France, giving Hitler's forces control of northern and western France, including Paris. A puppet government rules in the south.

13 August Battle of Britain begins over southern England, lasting until 15 September when Hitler abandons plans to invade Great Britain.

7 September Bombing raid on London marks the start of the Blitz on Britain.

27 September Germany, Japan and Italy agree the Tripartite Pact.

1941

22 June Start of Operation Barbarossa, Nazi invasion of the Soviet Union.

September Siege of Leningrad begins in Soviet Union.

7 December Japanese forces attack the US Navy base at Pearl Harbor, Hawaii, killing 2403 Americans. The United States declares war on Japan the next day. Germany and Italy declare war on the United States on 11 December.

1942

20 January At the Wannsee Conference, leading Nazis agree to carry out the systematic murder of millions of Jews in the Holocaust.

10 July American forces capture the island of Saipan after desperate Japanese resistance.

24 August Paris is liberated from German occupation.

1945

13-14 February Allied bombing of Dresden kills thousands of Germans in a firestorm, causing many people to question Allied bombing campaign.

19 February US Marines land on Japanese island of Iwo Jima, which is captured after fierce fighting.

30 April Death of Adolf Hitler.

4 June The Battle of Midway begins, in which the United States wins a decisive victory over the Japanese fleet.

November Allied forces win a major victory at the Battle of El Alamein in North Africa. The Red Army launches a major offensive against German forces at Stalingrad.

8 May Victory in Europe (VE) day following surrender of Germany.

6 August Americans explode first atomic bomb at Hiroshima Japan, followed three days later by atomic bomb at Nagasaki.

15 August Emperor of Japan surrenders.

1943

12 May Axis forces surrender in Tunisia, putting North Africa into Allied control.

5 July Battle of Kursk begins on Eastern Front, the largest land battle in history.

10 July Allied invasion of Sicily begins.

8 September Italy surrenders to the Allies, although German forces continue to fight in the country.

1944

21 January Allied forces land at Anzio, Italy, and attempt to capture Monte Cassino. The battle lasts for four months.

6 June D-Day landings on the beaches of Normandy.

GLOSSARY

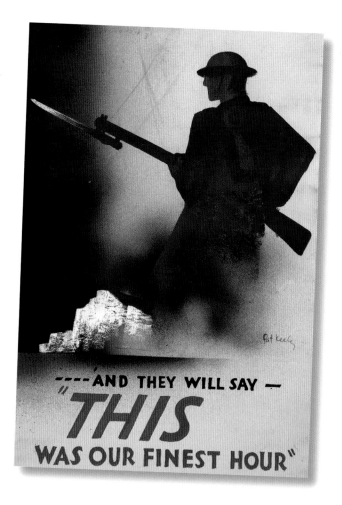

"----AND THEY WILL SAY ---- "THIS WAS OUR FINEST HOUR"

Allies countries fighting against Germany, Japan and the other Axis powers. After 1941, the Allies included Great Britain, the United States, the Soviet Union, Canada and many other countries

aristocrat member of a noble family

armistice agreement to end fighting in a war

Axis Germany, Japan, Italy (between 1940 and 1943) and their allies

capitalist economic and political system in which industries are controlled by private individuals rather than the state, generally with strong belief in individual freedom

colony land that is ruled from overseas, such as the colonies that made up the British Empire in 1939

communist economic and political system in which property and industries are controlled by the government, and everyone works for the state

conscription making it compulsory for people in a certain group to join the armed forces, such as all men between certain ages

convoy fleet of merchant ships accompanied by warships to protect them from attack

Mixed Metal Mania

Mixed Metal Mania

Solder, rivet, hammer, and wire exceptional jewelry

Kim St. Jean

KALMBACH BOOKS

Kalmbach Books

21027 Crossroads Circle
Waukesha, Wisconsin 53186
www.Kalmbach.com/Books

Please follow appropriate health and safety measures when working with torches. Some general guidelines are presented in this book, but always read and follow manufacturers' instructions. Every effort has been made to ensure the accuracy of the information presented; however, the publisher is not responsible for any injuries, losses, or other damages that may result from the use of the information in this book.

Published in 2011

17 16 15 14 13   3 4 5 6 7

Manufactured in the United States of America

ISBN: 978-0-87116-416-2

Publisher's Cataloging-In-Publication Data

St. Jean, Kim.

Mixed metal mania : solder, rivet, hammer, and wire exceptional jewelry / Kim St. Jean.

p. : ill. (chiefly col.) ; cm.

ISBN: 978-0-87116-416-2

1. Jewelry making—Handbooks, manuals, etc. 2. Art metal-work—Handbooks, manuals, etc. I. Title.

TT212 .S75 2011
739.274

Contents

Foreword

Long before we met Kim St. Jean, we heard glowing reports of her cold connections workshops from her students at William Holland School of Lapidary Arts. Our first opportunity to meet her occurred when our teaching schedules coincided at the school. We were immediately struck by Kim's vitality, inquisitive mind, and adventurous experimentation with new ideas and techniques. We knew we'd met a kindred spirit and fellow metal enthusiast. We then spent a week together as students in an enameling class. Kim impressed us with her bold, creative approach to enameling, showing utter fearlessness when it came to applying color. It was the perfect opportunity to observe her artistry at work.

Kim's educational training, experience, and dedication to her students is evident in the classroom in her well structured lessons and projects. She is extremely well-organized and in complete control as she uses a building-block approach to demonstrate each basic skill used in class projects, which encompass a variety of standard jewelry-making techniques. Kim willingly shares shortcuts and tips with her students—so it is no wonder they become her biggest fans after gaining knowledge in her classes and workshops as well as coming to enjoy working with metal and sharing in the creative process with her. Kim truly forms a permanent connection with her students and learns as much from them as she teaches them.

We are delighted to introduce you to our new friend and fellow metal-working enthusiast, Kim St. Jean, and her first book: *Mixed Metal Mania: solder, rivet, hammer, and wire exceptional jewelry*. Kim teaches at many venues where her classes are sold out to her faithful and enthusiastic followers. She has written this book to share with those who are unable to attend her workshops and as a handy reference for all. Kim's passion for embellishing metal is evident in her work, and her "What if?" attitude encourages her students to use her basic projects as stepping stones to blazing their own paths. You could say that Kim definitely puts her own stamp on her mixed metal creations.

Tom and Kay Benham
Contributing Editors, *Lapidary Journal Jewelry Artist*

Introduction

I have taught my metalworking style and techniques to well over a thousand students. Often, as I am explaining something, I hear, "do you have a book about this?" I also hear, "You explained that in a way I finally understood." I attribute this to my background as an early childhood educator. I often had to come up with unique ways to explain things when the students didn't grasp a concept. I devour books on jewelry design and techniques, I love taking classes, and I absolutely cherish the times when I can sit and create with peers. My passion for learning converged with my passion to teach, and presto … here I am, living my dream.

The casual observer of my home library can tell at a glance which books are my favorites: They're the ones with the tabs sticking out marking pages that I return to over and over. This is what I hope this book will become for you. I envision you happily working away on a project of your own design and referring back to this book for reinforcement.

Mixed Metal Mania is divided into five sections. First, I explain tools and techniques. This is a long section with lots of detail. Some of what's covered may be familiar to you, and some might be brand new. It's OK to dip in and out, and learn what you need to know before moving on. This section should be your "go to" place for clarification or explanation.

Four project chapters reinforce the basics. Every project has been tested with students and was developed to teach and practice a specific skill. I hope you like the designs, but it is the skills and techniques perfected in making the projects that are important. If you master what I'm teaching, you'll open the door to endless creativity.

The first set of projects is dedicated to building your comfort with tools. The second group uses more skills and introduces additional tools. The third collection adds the magic of fire, and the final set combines multiple techniques and advanced tools resulting in more complex (and rewarding!) jewelry.

Tools

Tools for metalworking can be divided into two categories: need to have, and nice to have. This section is intended to give you a better understanding of a wide range of tools and how they are used. Please don't rush out and buy everything listed here. I have been acquiring tools for a long time!

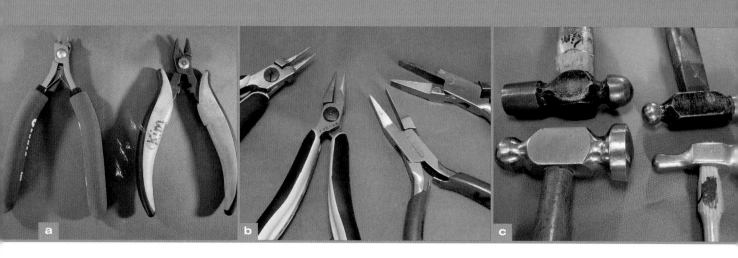

My opinion about tools: Use what feels comfortable and will get the job done correctly. I happen to like used tools. I love the hunt for old tools as much as I love the tools themselves. They are treasures to me. Although I should have what I need by now, I continue to discover new tools on an almost daily basis. I am a self-proclaimed tool junkie. Why don't you come on in to my studio! Let's take a look at my bench.

What you'll see right on top of everything are my pliers. I have a pair of razor flush cutters and a pair of what I call "sacrificial cutters" **(a)**. These are a chipped and dinged version of my favorite cutters. I use them for cutting tacks, nails and mystery metals that I don't want to risk using my good cutters on. I have a pair of roundnose pliers, chainnose pliers, and two identical pairs of flatnose pliers **(b)**. A four-ounce ball-peen hammer, a domed chasing hammer, a two-ounce chasing hammer, and a two-ounce ball-peen hammer are close at hand **(c)**, along with my center punches, medium stepped forming pliers, spring-loaded punch, and nylon jaw bracelet-bending pliers **(d)**. I keep my files in two water bottle ice trays **(e)**. These keep the files standing up so they are easy to see, and separated so they don't touch each other and become damaged. My jeweler's saw is hanging off my bench pin with my beeswax close by **(f)**. I keep my saw blades in throat-culture tubes labeled by size. I use a two-pound anvil for most of my work. I like to do my stamping on the bottom of an antique iron **(g)**. Take a look over at my hammers. There's a planishing hammer, bordering hammer, and a weighted rawhide mallet strapped with one of my husband's old belts to the tree stump **(h)**. Did you notice that tree stump? A tree stump is the most efficient work surface for hammering metal. It's dense and you receive little vibration or kick-back when hammering. With a stump as a work surface, you can work twice as effectively as on a table top, and best of

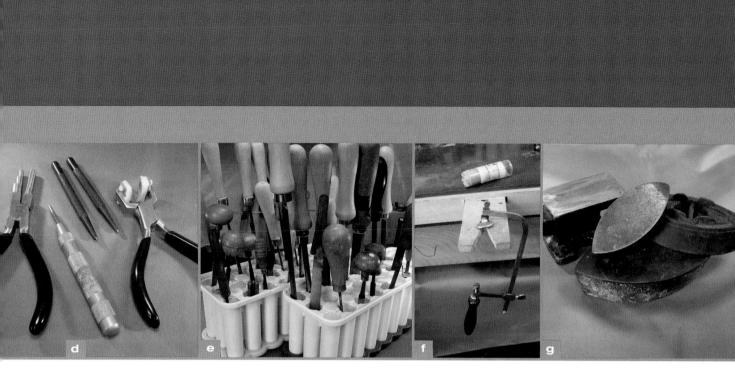

all ... they are usually free! The rest of my hammers are nearby on the table. Hammers and files are my weakness. I love to find unusual hammers at flea markets and antique stores. Each old hammer has its own unique fingerprint. My favorites change on a daily basis. I have a piece of railroad track on my stump that makes a perfect anvil. Placing heavy magnets on it will reduce the "pinging" noise that comes when hammering. Across the room is a stand with a rolling mill on it **(i)**. Beside the rolling mill is another table with my drill press,

buffing machine, and tumbler. I keep my flex shaft and two other Dremel-type tools hanging on an old I.V. bottle rack with wheels so that I can move them around **(j)**. Under each table there are gray tubs full of steel wool, sanding sponges, wire, stencils, miscellaneous tools, disk cutter set, stamps, doming blocks, scrap metal, and chemicals. I also have several bins with my hoarded treasures that will someday be worked into projects **(k)**. You'll see that my soldering equipment is also on my bench. I use a Solderite

solder board, pick, cross locking tweezers, and pickle pot. I have an oxygen- propane Smith Little Torch and an air-acetylene torch **(l)**. When needed, I pull out the annealing pan filled with pumice stones.

I have to say, I'm quite proud of my studio. But believe me, it didn't all come overnight. I've been collecting these tools for years.

Now I'd like to tell you a little more detail about the tools you'll be using and how to use them:

Cutters Use fine, flush diagonal cutters for close- up cutting and keep a pair of "sacrificial" cutters for cutting mystery metals, iron, and steel.

Pliers You must have chainnose pliers, roundnose pliers, and two pairs of flat- nose pliers. Pliers are used in every project we'll do.

Wire gauges and calipers Measure the diameter of wire and beads with these **(m**, page 10**)**.

Files and Cratex wheels If you can have only one file, get a #2 cut barrette file, but you'll want more. I have triangular files in all sizes to get into small

Tools

spaces, and other files in different cuts and shapes to smooth metal inside and on the edges. A flex shaft or other power tool is the most effective for filing. Equip the flex shaft with a Cratex rubberized abrasive wheel. Its three shapes enable you to reach inside angles, flares, and grooves **(n)**. There are different grades of Cratex abrasives. The red-brown wheel is a fine-grade abrasive used to remove burs, metal around the edge of a bezel, or heavy scratches. The blue wheel is finer, and removes marks or a small amount of metal.

Sanding sponges
Sanding sponges round the edges of textured metals. Buy coarse sanding sponges and cut them into thirds for easier handling and less waste. Sand from the center of the piece down over the edge on all sides **(o)**. Then, flip and repeat on the back.

Specialty pliers Nylon jaw pliers straighten wire, remove kinks from thin gauge wire, and fold over prongs. They can be a substitute for chainnose or flatnose pliers when you don't want to mar the material you're working with. Nylon jaw bracelet-bending pliers

form gentle curves in metal without marking it. They are often used with or instead of a bracelet mandrel **(p)**.

Shears I do most of my cutting with shears. I use a pair of inexpensive bonsai tree trimming shears. They are slim and comfortable **(q)** You can also purchase professional kitchen shears such as Joyce Chen's.

Jeweler's saw A good starting place is with a 4-in. saw frame and 3/0 and 2/0 blades **(r)**.

Spring-loaded punch
Use a spring-loaded punch to dimple metal before using any power tool to drill holes. With a punched

dimple as your guide, you'll feel the drill slide into the dimple, and you won't have to struggle to see an ink or scribe mark **(s)**.

Center punch set Use these to flare tube rivets **(t)**.

Forming pliers Sold under the brand name Wrap 'n' Tap, these are available in three sizes. Medium is perfect for jump rings, ear wires, shepherds hook clasps, and bails. I love this tool! The medium barrels are 5, 7, and 10 mm in diameter. Use larger forming pliers (13, 16 and 20 mm barrels) for rings. The smaller pair, also called multi-size looping pliers, has

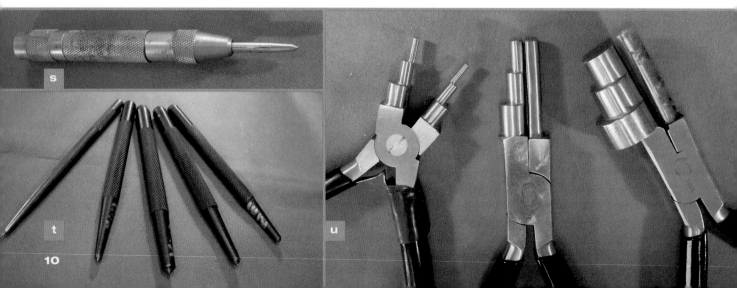

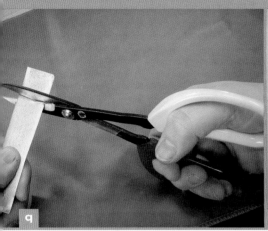

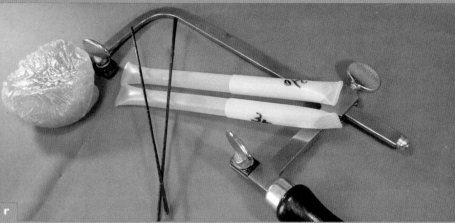

2–9 mm barrels. Use it for making jump rings **(u)**.

Flex shaft Sand and drill with a flex shaft. It is a staple at most jeweler's benches. It is the workhorse of tools—it significantly reduces hand-filing time. The handle is attached to a flexible shaft which is attached to a motor that suspends above your work station. You can use this tool in water and hard-to-reach places. Control the motor speed with a foot pedal **(v)**.

Ring clamp If your hand cramps easily or it is difficult for you to grasp small parts, use a ring clamp to hold a piece while you are filing, or when you are using a power tool and the metal begins to get hot **(w)**.

Marking tools Use a fine-point permanent marker to mark shapes to cut, notes to yourself, directional arrows, or anything you want on metal. The ink will disappear when the metal is heated to soldering temperature or pickled. If any mark remains, clean it off with nail polish remover. For exact work, use a scribe to scratch marks in the metal. The fine mark can be buffed off.

Vise A 4-in. swivel clamp-on vise is useful near the bench for holding a tube cutting jig to cut tubing, holding material for filing or braiding, or sawing jump rings. I use a larger 10-pound bench vise secured on a stump to hold material for some forms in foldforming.

Tube-cutting jig This tool holds tubing so you can use a jeweler's saw to make a clean, perpendicular cut to make a tube rivet. The jig has an extending measuring arm. Push the tubing out to the measuring arm to cut uniform lengths.

Pipe cutter Use a pipe cutter **(x)** to cut copper, brass, aluminum, or sterling tubing. If you are a plumber or live with one, you use this tool all the time. Clamp the cutter on the pipe loosely, turn the pipe, and then tighten the cutter slightly and turn again. Don't over-tighten the cutter. Continue scoring the tube until it finally snaps off. Sometimes on small tubing or pipe made from any metal, or on sterling tubing of any size, the cutter pinches the tube closed. In this case, I prefer a jeweler's saw to a pipe cutter because it is much more precise.

Drill press This is my personal favorite tool for making holes **(y)**.

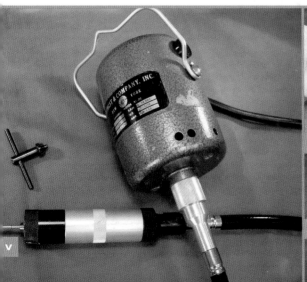

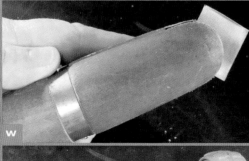

Kim's Unconventional Tools

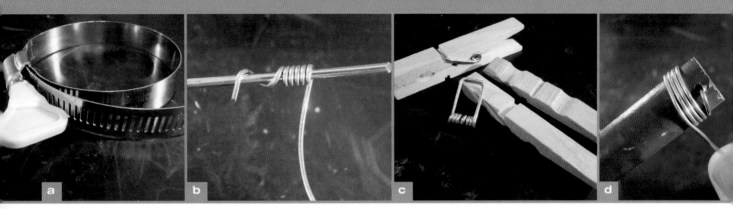

The following are some of my favorite tools. These are not tools that you will find at any jewelry supplier. These are everyday items that I have modified to use in my designing process and in making my projects. Don't laugh until you try them.

RV sewer-hose clamp

This resembles a dryer hose clamp with one exception: This hose clamp has a knob so you can easily adjust the clamp's circumference. The hose clamp, along with a tape measure, makes a great bangle-bracelet gauge. Tighten the knob until you have a circle you can pull your hand through, but still have a snug fit. Measure the outside circumference of the clamp and you'll know how much metal to cut **(a)**.

Bicycle spoke

Cut the ends off a 14-gauge spoke and you have a perfect mandrel for coiling wire **(b)**.

Clothespin

Remove the spring from a wooden clothespin for two great bezel pushers. I love these because I don't have to worry about scratching or chipping my stones while pushing the bezel over the edge **(c)**. I also use one to hold my metal when I hammer to protect my fingers.

Carpenters pencils

Use carpenters pencils as dowels to make oval jump rings. Drill a 1⁄16-in. hole in one end of the pencil, insert the wire end, and then coil the wire around the pencil, tape it, and saw **(d)**.

Antique irons

My favorite bench block is the bottom of an antique iron. I have three of them, one large, one medium, and one child size. They are not as loud as a conventional bench block. They are handy for flattening metal pieces: Place the metal piece on the iron, use a smaller iron as a "clapper," and tap on the metal to flatten it. I also use my irons to straighten and work-harden my wire—cut a length of wire and roll it between two irons **(e)**.

Large horse-hair artist paintbrush

I constantly use a large horse-hair artist's brush to keep filing debris off of my work surface. Any large paintbrush will work **(f)**.

Sheet metal and welder's pliers

I use sheet metal and welder's pliers as a 90-degree bending break. The pliers have large jaws for grabbing a whole strip of metal. I have them in 3-in. and 8-in. sizes. They are great for making crisp, tight corners and edges **(g)**.

Jump ring sawing block

Use a 1 x 1-in. piece of wood cut 3 in. long. Saw a wedge and screw a piece of Plexiglas to one side. Saw a slit down the side of

the Plexiglas to the bottom of the wedge in the block. Attach a piece of leather to the top. To use the block, thread the jeweler's saw blade through a coil of wire. Put the coil in the wedge and saw down the slit in the Plexiglas. To keep the coil still, hold it in place with the leather as you saw **(h)**.

Sanding wedge Use a 2 x 3 in. piece of wood cut 3 in. long to prop metal while filing **(i)**.

Liver of sulfur solution Rinse out an opaque plastic bottle like a hydrogen peroxide bottle. Fill it with water and add about six pea-sized lumps of liver of sulfur **(j)** and shake. Replace and tighten the cap. To use: Pour about ¼ in. of the solution into a jar and add water in a one-to-one ratio. Re-fill the plastic bottle with water. Continue to do this until the day when the liver of sulfur solution is very light yellow. Then, add six more lumps of liver of sulfur. This will extend the life of your liver of sulfur and save you some dollars!

Agitator for ferric chloride Ferric chloride etching solution works better if it is warm and is agitated during the etching process. Place your etching bowl on your dryer while you are doing laundry. The heat and movement of the dryer will accelerate the etching process. Alternatively, place the etching bowl on a TV tray with a running tumbler.

Paper cutter a paper cutter from the discount hardware store **(k)** can be used like metal shears to cut up to 20-gauge copper, silver, and other nonferrous metals. The paper guide allows cutting straight perpendicular cuts. They aren't always perfectly perpendicular, but they can be easily cleaned up with a file. This type of cutter uses a sharp-edged piece of steel to cut in place of a blade. Be careful—you can still cut yourself!

Steel binding wire Use steel binding wire to shape small props for your pieces while you are soldering; my friend Nancy calls this "furniture" **(l)**.

Drill bit to remove burs A large drill bit can remove burs after drilling. Twist a drill bit that is larger than the hole drilled to remove the bur caused by the original drill bit **(m)**.

Bicycle spoke soldering pick Cut the ends from a bicycle spoke and cut the spoke in half. Drill a hole in a wooden dowel, insert the spoke, file the end, and you've got a soldering pick. It's not the best, but it's inexpensive. If your solder sticks to the end, file it off **(n)**.

Chicken feeder Hold your pliers upright with a sliding top chicken feeder on your work table **(o)**.

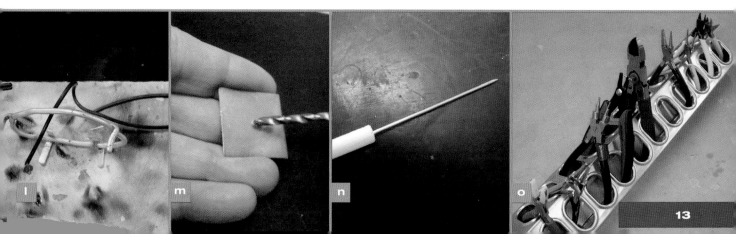

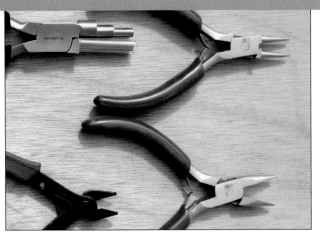

Wire wrapping clockwise from top right: roundnose pliers, chainnose pliers (these have a smooth inner jaw), close-cutting wire cutters, stepped pliers (Wrap 'n' Tap).

Cold connection Clockwise from top left: anvil, hole-punching pliers, wire cutters, coarse sanding sponge, two-hole punch, spring-loaded punch, file, ball-peen hammer.

Foldforming vise, hammers (bordering, weighted rawhide mallet, ball peen, etc.) oyster knife or dull kitchen knife, annealing pan, torch, pickle, pickle pot, rinse bowl, copper tongs, optional rolling mill.

Sawing (clockwise from top left) beeswax, saw frame, 3/0 and 2/0 blades, bench pin, vise or clamp.

Stamping and texturing ruler, texturing hammer, ball-peen hammer, letter stamps, anvil, texture stamps, paper, pencil.

Measurement Conversion Chart

Multiply	...by	...to find
Inches	2.54	centimeters
Centimeters	.4	inches
Feet	30.5	centimeters
Centimeters	.03	feet
Yards	.9	meters
Meters	1.1	yards
Ounces	28.3	grams
Grams	.035	ounces

Soldering pickle pot with pickle; torch; flux; copper tongs; solder board; locking tweezers; pick; sheers; chip solder; extra easy, easy, medium, and hard solder paste; brass brush; dental floss.

Patina (liver of sulfer) lidded jar, liver of sulfer solution and pellets, candle warmer, tweezers, rinse bowl and water, 0000 steel wool, paintbrush.

Kim's Studio Tool Checklist
Make copies of this checklist to get your tools organized for each project or use as a shopping wish list.

Need to have:
- ❑ roundnose pliers
- ❑ chainnose pliers
- ❑ nylon-jaw pliers
- ❑ 2 pairs flatnose pliers
- ❑ flush cutters
- ❑ heavy-duty flush cutters
- ❑ blunt knife
- ❑ metal shears
- ❑ bench block
- ❑ small (2 lb.) anvil
- ❑ 4 oz. ball-peen hammer
- ❑ 8 oz. ball-peen hammer
- ❑ domed chasing hammer
- ❑ rawhide mallet
- ❑ soft blow mallet
- ❑ bracelet mandrel
- ❑ ring mandrel
- ❑ jeweler's saw frame
- ❑ 2/0 and 3/0 saw blades
- ❑ beeswax
- ❑ wooden bench pin
  vises
- ❑ third hand
- ❑ files
- ❑ coarse sanding sponges
- ❑ soft bristle brass brush
- ❑ Solderite soldering board
- ❑ soldering pick
- ❑ 2400°F butane torch
- ❑ cross-locking tweezers
- ❑ crock pot
- ❑ candle warmer
- ❑ plastic containers
- ❑ towels
- ❑ spring-loaded punch
- ❑ hand punch set

- ❑ center punches
- ❑ variety of dapping blocks
- ❑ variety of daps
- ❑ sketchbook
- ❑ notebook
- ❑ pencils
- ❑ markers
- ❑ metal ruler
- ❑ tripod

Nice to have:
- ❑ large stepped pliers
- ❑ medium stepped pliers
- ❑ bracelet-bending pliers
- ❑ Cindy's bender
- ❑ disk cutter
- ❑ acetylene B torch setup
  with #1 and #3 tips
- ❑ Smith Little Torch
- ❑ rolling mill
- ❑ bordering hammer
- ❑ letter stamps
- ❑ texture stamps
- ❑ texture plates
- ❑ flex shaft
- ❑ Dremel-style tool
- ❑ Cratex wheels and
  mandrels
- ❑ rubber work surface
- ❑ tree stump with belt strap
- ❑ variety of hammers
- ❑ forming stakes
- ❑ hydraulic press
- ❑ ring clamp
- ❑ drill press
- ❑ rubber block
- ❑ hole punches

Basic Techniques

Cold Connections

A cold connection joins two or more metals without using solders or glues.

Wire-wrapped loop

This wrap can be used in earrings, chain, and as a cold connection. Every artist has his or her own twist—pun intended—to making wire-wrapped loops. My version works best for me. If you've been making loops differently, stick with it if it works for you. If you are struggling with the method, though, or would just like to try a new way, give my version a go.

Tools
- roundnose pliers
- chainnose pliers
- wire cutters

Materials
- wire of any type, any gauge

1. Hold roundnose pliers in your non-dominant hand (i.e. if you are right handed, in your left hand). Hold chainnose pliers in your dominant hand (i.e. if you are right handed, in your right hand). Hold both pliers horizontally **(a)**.
2. Grasp a length of wire with roundnose pliers leaving at least a 1-in. tail **(b)**.
3. Using the end of chainnose pliers, grasp the very tip of the wire tail **(c)**.
4. Bring the wire straight down towards you, creating a 90-degree bend **(d)**.

5. Pull the wire all the way down so that it is pointing to the ground **(e)**.
6. Swing the wire back up and away from you so that it is snug up against the bottom of the roundnose pliers and is now extending straight out and away from your body **(f)**.
7. Use chainnose pliers to wrap the wire tail around the wire that is extending from the roundnose pliers. Make as many wraps as desired, and make them as close to each other and as neat as desired **(g)**.
8. With both sets of pliers remaining on the wire, gently twist your non-dominant hand up about 45 degrees so that your loop will be at a 90-degree angle to the remaining wire.
9. Release the wire from both sets of pliers and use wire cutters to gently snip off the remaining wire. Tuck any wire snug to the wraps, using chainnose pliers.

*Photos **a–g** show how to make a wire-wrapped loop on the end of a wire. For a dangle, string a bead on a headpin and make a wire-wrapped loop above the bead **(h)**.

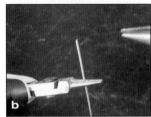
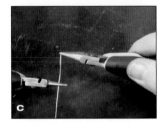
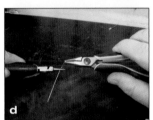

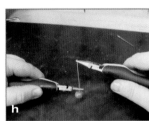

Prepping binding wire

Annealed steel binding wire is a great-looking material for jewelry design, but it presents both drawbacks and perks. First the drawbacks: Steel wire can be covered with residue, and it is prone to rust. It must be prepared before it is used. The perks are that it is readily available in hardware stores, it is inexpensive, and it creates an interesting, organic-looking result.

Prepare the wire:
1. Cut a length of wire.
2. Run it through a piece of 0000 steel wool **(a)** several times.
3. Seal with a microcrystalline wax such as Renaissance wax **(b)**.

Rivets

A rivet is a metal pin used as a connector. A rivet can be as plain as a wire or as complex as a fancy nail with a vintage design on top **(a)**. Rivets come in several forms: the basic rivet, the nail-head rivet, and the tube rivet. The process of connecting two pieces of metal with a rivet is called riveting, so the word is both a noun and a verb. The most important thing to remember when riveting is hole size. If the hole in your piece of metal is too big, the rivet will not spread out over the top layer of metal. If your hole is too small, you can't insert the rivet.

TIP Here's how to solve the problem of the hole size not matching the rivet size. The lesser of two evils is the hole being too small. To solve, you can either file the rivet down, or gently enlarge the hole with a round file. On the other hand, if your rivet hole is too large, you can gently tap the hole with the balled side of a small ball-peen hammer or chasing hammer, you can tap the hole with the round end of a dapping punch, or you can use a washer threaded onto the rivet to equalize the size of the hole. This last suggestion is very useful when using found objects that may already have holes in them (for instance, a vintage watch part).

To have a successful rivet connection, you must know

the size of your rivet material. If you are using wire, you need to know the gauge **(b)**. Choose a drill bit or other hole making device that is the same size as the wire. If you don't have a perfect match, err on the side of having your wire slightly larger than the hole and then taper the wire end. You need a really snug fit for a rivet to work. For example, to make a ⅟₁₆-in. rivet, use 14-gauge wire, file one end to a point, and force that end into the ⅟₁₆-in. hole. When the wire is in as far as it will go, trim the end and continue with the riveting process **(c)**. The rule for a proportionate rivet is to cut it to a length equal to half the diameter of the hole, which is also half the thickness of the wire. For example, the silver handle side of a two-hole punch makes a ⅟₁₆-in. hole. If you use 16-gauge wire, the length of the rivet sticking out of the hole on one side is roughly 1 mm, and the overall length of the rivet should be a little less than 2 mm. (I discovered that a gift card is 2 mm thick. I use one as a gauge by punching a ⅟₁₆-in. hole in the corner, sliding it over the rivet, and then cutting.) Trim the wire with flush cutters while it is in the hole, then gently file the top **(d, e)**. Filing serves two purposes: First, it removes any burs left by the cutters providing a flat surface to work with,

and second, it begins the spreading process of the rivet. After trimming, it's time to hammer. I use a small 4 oz. ball-peen hammer to spread rivets. Picture the rivet as a compass. Begin by gently tapping the southern edge of the rivet with the flat side of the hammer twice, then move to the north and tap twice. Tap west twice and then

east twice. Flip the piece over and repeat on the other side. Continue this pattern until the rivet has spread out over the sheet metal. To soften the edges, use the rounded side of the hammer and gently tap the edges all the way around the rivet. This domes the rivet, making the side gradually slope down to the metal **(f)**.

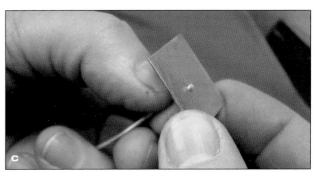
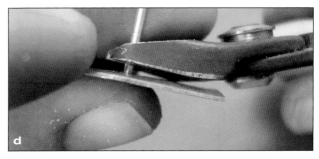

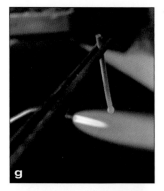

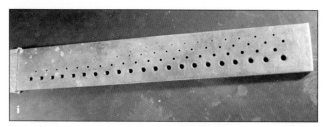

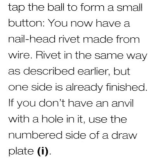

Nail-head rivets

Nail-head rivets can be anything that will spread over two or more pieces of metal: tacks, framing nails, micro screws, or even purchased aluminum rivets. To make a nail-head rivet out of wire, cut a 1-in. piece of copper, silver, gold, or gold-filled wire in the appropriate gauge. Hold the wire with tweezers at a 90-degree angle at the tip of the blue flame of a torch. Flash the wire up and down in the flame to gently heat the whole wire, and then let it rest at the tip of the blue flame. The wire end will ball up **(g)** just like when making a headpin (see page 35). Pickle or file off the fire scale. I have drilled a hole in my little anvil just for making rivets. I place the balled wire in the hole **(h)** and gently

tap the ball to form a small button: You now have a nail-head rivet made from wire. Rivet in the same way as described earlier, but one side is already finished. If you don't have an anvil with a hole in it, use the numbered side of a draw plate **(i)**.

Tube rivets

A tube rivet can be made of any metal tubing that can be flared out over another piece of metal—copper, aluminum, silver, and brass tubing are good choices. The same rules apply to tube rivets as to wire or nail-head rivets. The size of the hole must be the same as the diameter of the tube being used. The length of the tube should be half the diameter of the tube or hole. The easiest way to cut

tubing is with a tube-cutting jig and a jeweler's saw. (Tube cutters are not designed to cut the very small tubing we mostly use in jewelry design.) Seamless sterling silver 2 x 3 mm crimp tubes from your local bead store **(j)** are a simple solution for connecting 24-gauge sheet metal. Use a two-hole punch to make a 3/32-in. hole (the size of the 2 x 3 mm crimp tube). Place the tube upright on the anvil. Set a small nail in the top and tap very gently with a small hammer **(k)** to flare out the tube **(l)**. Turn the tube over, slide the metal down over the tube, and flare the other side of the tube. Gently tap down the edges with a hammer **(m)**. You can also use an eyelet from the scrapbooking section of a

craft store as a tube rivet. Determine the size of the eyelet and coordinate the size of hole in your metal. Most commercial eyelets are 1/8 in. You can flare an eyelet with a commercially purchased spring-loaded eyelet setter, or you can flare an eyelet with a nail-set punch. If you choose to use a spring-loaded eyelet setter, the back of the eyelet will split open and look like a flower of sorts **(n)**. A nail set done with a hammer will curl down the edges so that if done correctly, both front and back will look the same.

Staples, tabs, and prongs

These are all similar cold-connection attachments. They can be made of wire, or elaborately cut out of sheet metal using a jeweler's saw. An example of a staple cold connection is the elaborate wrought-iron balconies of New Orleans. Tabs are commonly used to hold the glass in a picture frame, and prongs are used to set stones **(o)**.

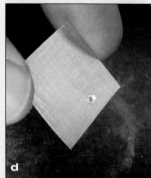

How to set a tube rivet

Tools
- bench block
- punch
- jeweler's saw
- tube cutting jig
- file
- small hammer
- drill or hole punch

Materials
- copper, aluminum, brass or silver tubing
- sheet metal

TIP When purchasing tubing, remember that it is identified by the inside diameter.

1. Punch the appropriate sized hole in the metal to fit your tube rivet **(a)**.
2. Cut the tube to the appropriate length. Use the same formula as the nail-head rivet or use 2 mm x 3 mm seamless sterling silver crimp tubes **(b)**.
3. Stand the tube on the bench block. Place a dap slightly larger than the opening on the top of the tube and gently tap with a very light hammer to flare the edges. Be careful not to split your tube **(c)**.
4. Turn the flared tube upside down on the bench block and place your metals to be joined on top **(d)**.
6. Using the same dap, flare the other end of the tube **(e)**.
7. Gently tap the flared lip down over the metals **(f)**.

Lashing

This connection uses fine wire as if it's thread. You simply sew or knot the metal together. I've borrowed my method from embroidery stitching I learned from my grandmother and macramé knotting I learned from my mom.

Tools
- drill or hole punch
- close-cutting wire cutters
- chainnose pliers
- spring-loaded punch

Supplies
- 26- or 28-gauge copper, sterling silver, gold, or craft wire
- sheet metal to connect

1. Mark and drill two holes in each metal piece. File all the burs.
2. Cut at least 4 in. of wire. More wire will make a bulkier lash, which can be a pleasing design element.
3. Sew into the first hole from the back of the metal, leaving a ¼-in. tail. **(a)**.
4. Bend the tail flat to the back and hold it in place with your non-dominant hand. Sew down through the second hole from front to back **(b)**.
5. Continue sewing the wire through the holes. I like using a wire gauge that lets me make three or more passes through each hole. I like the wispy look.
6. End the sewing on the back by looping the working end under the bridge built in Step 5 **(c–e)**.
7. Pull the wire as close and tight to the wires and metal as possible. Repeat twice.
10. Repeat with the tail created in Step 4 **(f)**. Trim the remaining wire and pinch down any sharp edges **(g)**.

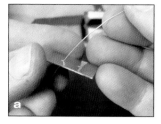

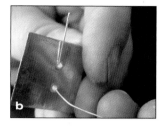

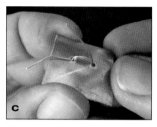

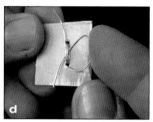

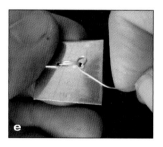

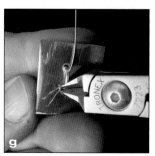

Sawing

Mention using a jeweler's saw and most people cringe. I felt the same way at first. You have to learn to embrace the jeweler's saw, or as I like to say, "become one with the saw." When done correctly, sawing metal can be quite relaxing. It's sort of a jeweler's Zen. The most important things to remember are: Use the correct size saw blade, don't hold the saw in a death grip, and move the metal—not the saw—as you cut curves. If you can remember these three things, you will become a jeweler's saw enthusiast like me.

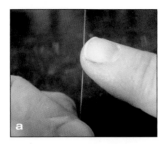
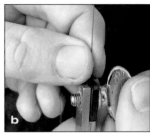
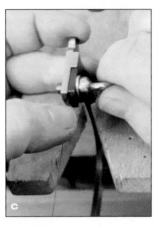

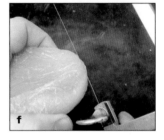

Tools
- Jeweler's saw (I prefer a 4 in.)
- 2/0 or 3/0 saw blades
- Beeswax or other lubricant
- V-slot bench pin

A jeweler's saw blade is a very thin strip of metal with teeth running down one side. The projects in this book use 3/0 or 2/0 saw blades to work mostly with 24-gauge sheet metal.

TIP To confirm the blade is the right size for the metal, check that three blade teeth are on the metal at all times. If your blade is too large it will jump on the metal; if it is too small, it will break easily.

For a proper fit into the frame, determine the direction of the blade's teeth. Hold the blade in front of you and (if you have really good eyesight) you will see the teeth. They should be facing down, like half of an evergreen tree. If you—like me—can no longer see the teeth, run a finger up the blade **(a)**. If you can feel the teeth, the blade is facing in the right direction. In other words, you're running your finger against the grain and the teeth feel sharp.

Now that you've verified the correct cutting edge, you're ready to put the blade in the saw frame. Loosen both of the nuts on the handle side of the frame **(b)**. Prop the frame against the table and the handle against your abdomen. Insert the blade in the bottom slot with the teeth up. Lean in toward the table, putting the saw frame in a bind. Insert the other end of the blade and tighten the nut **(c)**. Lean back, the frame releases, and the blade is in tight. To be certain, pluck the blade **(d)**. You should hear a nice "ping." If you get a "thunk," try again. Your blade isn't tight enough.

Use a V-slot bench pin for sawing. A bench pin is a 1 x 4-in. piece of wood with a V-shaped slot sawed out that is secured to a table with a C-clamp **(e)**. Position the bench pin directly in front of you, preferably at chest height. Lubricate the blade with beeswax **(f)**. Repeat often; it will make your sawing easier and prolong the life of your blade. Sit up straight and hold the saw at a 90-degree angle. Don't hold the handle tightly. I cannot emphasize this enough!

If you hold the saw in a death grip, you will break your blades and you won't be able to saw smoothly. Think cocktail hour—pinky out! Grasp the handle with your fingertips **(g)**. The blade's teeth run down the edge about 4 in. Use all the teeth. Make smooth strokes and fluid and graceful wrist motions, up and down like playing a violin—well, I've never played a violin, but that's how I imagine it. The blade cuts on the down stroke, so start your sawing with a downward pull. Once you have the blade moving up and down in the metal, place the middle finger of your non-dominant hand in front of the blade and place your

index finger behind the blade to securely hold the metal while you saw **(h)**. When it's necessary to make a turn or curve, continue moving the saw blade up and down at a 90-degree angle and

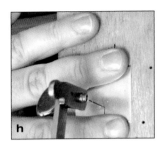

turn the metal with your non-dominant hand. If you try to twist or turn the blade, it will break. If you get into a spot where you need to come back out, continue sawing up and down and back your way out. If the blade is not moving, it will stick in the metal and break. To saw negative space, first drill a hole in the metal. Loosen the top nut of the saw frame, release the blade, and insert the blade in the hole with your pattern facing up **(i)**. Reinsert the saw blade following the same directions as before. You won't get as nice of a "ping" now because the metal on the blade flattens the sound, but you should feel the same tension in the blade as before. Begin sawing **(j)**.

Practice, practice, practice! Sawing is not perfected on the first try!

How to use a disk cutter

The disk cutter punches round disks out of metal sheet. If you've ever tried to use shears or a jeweler's saw to cut a perfect circle, you know what I mean when I say the disk cutter is an awesome tool. It cuts sheet up to 18-gauge and disks up to 1 in. in diameter. (If you're cutting disks larger than 1 in., use a hydraulic press.)

Place the bottom half of the disk cutter on a rubber mat on a solid surface. Place the metal sheet on your desired hole size **(a)**. Place the top half of the disk cutter on top of the metal **(b)**. Select the appropriate size cutting dap and put it in the slot, making sure that the cutting edge is facing down. Use a 3-lb. sledge or dead blow brass hammer to strike the cutting die **(c)**. Hold the disk cutter steady with your non-dominant hand and strike the die with two or three blows **(d)**. Make sure that your non-dominant hand is not covering the space between the two layers of metal because it could get pinched during the cutting process. The fewer blows you strike, the cleaner your disk will be cut **(e)**. This is why you need a heavy hammer.

How to cut a tube rivet

The most efficient way to cut a tube is with a jeweler's saw. Unfortunately, in jewelry design, we work in very small scale. It is very difficult to cut a tiny tube while holding it on a bench pin. Never fear: There is a very handy tool called a tube cutting jig. Hold the tube cutting jig in your non-dominant hand and saw with your dominant hand—or lock the jig in a vise and use the jeweler's saw, freeing up your non-dominant hand to steady the tube. The really nice thing about the tube cutting jig is that once you have the length set, you can cut out multiples of the same length, which is helpful for a project like making hinges.

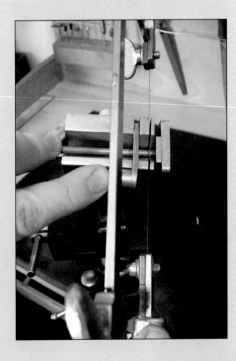

Making Holes

Insignificant? Not at all. Holes are a very important part of metalworking. There are several options for making holes in metal.

Drill press While there is no one perfect hole-making tool, my favorite is the drill press **(a)**. You don't need a huge, expensive drill press. Mine is a small table-top model from a discount tool store. A drill press can drill through thick metals, multiple metals, coins, glass, stone, found objects, and more. The table can be adjusted to accommodate any size or shape you are drilling. There are several projects in this book that will be difficult to do if you do not have a drill press.

The first step in using a drill press is to set the speed. Set the belts on the drill press so that the bit is going about 1100 rpms. This is slow enough that you can almost see the grooves in the bit spiraling down **(b)**. Once you have the press going at the right speed, you want to make sure the table—a stand attached to the drill base that can be raised and lowered as needed—is at the correct level. You don't want the drill bit to have to travel a long way to make contact with the metal, because you might have trouble aligning the bit to the dimple. Set the table so there is about ¼ in. between the metal and the bottom of the drill bit **(c)**. Always have a scrap piece of wood between the metal and the table. Never drill directly into the metal on the table. Before using any type of power tool to make a hole in metal, use a spring-loaded punch or a center punch to dimple the spot that you intend to drill so the drill bit can make purchase in the metal. Otherwise the bit will skitter across the metal making unwanted marks. If you continue to apply pressure, the drill bit will most likely break. To drill a hole, hold the metal in place with the peace sign fingers of your non-dominant hand. Make sure that the dimple in the metal is directly below the drill bit. Turn the drill on and slowly bring the bit down to the metal, watching it make contact. Begin drilling. Keep the drill press running as the bit goes in the metal and as you pull the bit out. If you let go of the metal and it begins to spin, turn the drill press off and let it come to a stop. Bring the bit down to the wood, reestablish your grip and turn the drill back on. It is now safe to pull the bit out of the metal.

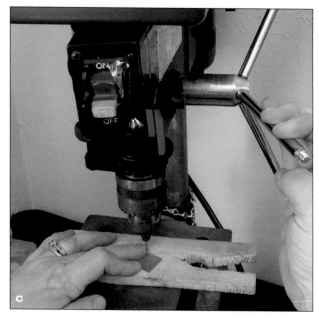

Two-hole punch This commercial tool is sold through jewelry tool suppliers. It makes 1/16- or 3/32-in. holes in up to 24-gauge metal. This tool, in a sense, standardized the popular size of rivets used in cold connections today. The silver handle on one side makes a 1/16-in. hole that accommodates a 16-gauge wire rivet. The black handle makes a 3/32-in. hole that accommodates a 2 x 3 mm tube rivet. Position the metal in the slot underneath the handle and begin screwing it down. The punch will eventually pierce through. To remove the metal, unscrew the handle until the metal is released **(d)**. The disadvantage to this tool is a limited work area due to the "reach" of the punch.

Hole punch pliers These are comfortable to hold and are easy to use, but have several drawbacks: There is a limited work area, they will only pierce up to 20-gauge metal, and each pair of pliers makes only one hole size. To use the pliers, line the metal up under the tooth and squeeze down until the tooth pops out the other side **(e)**. To remove the metal from the tooth, gently twist the metal until it comes off.

Flex shaft
A flex shaft is handy in metalworking. It's easy to drill holes with one, but if you're not careful you'll end up with burned fingers and frustration. The key to using a flex shaft is to remember to go very slowly. When you engage the motor, you should be able to see the groove of the drill bit turn. If you go too fast, the drill bit cannot make purchase in the metal and will only cause friction. Practice using a flex shaft to learn how much pressure to apply with the hand piece and what speed it takes to drill through your metal of choice. Hold the flex shaft in your dominant hand in a fist grip **(f)**. Hold the metal on a bench pin or wood scrap with the peace-sign fingers of your non-dominant hand. Position the drill bit in the dimple for your hole. Gently press the foot pedal down until the drill bit just barely begins turning. Gently apply pressure with the hand piece. If the metal becomes hot, the drill bit is moving too fast; back off the foot pedal. Drill through the metal and continue as you pull the drill bit out of the metal.

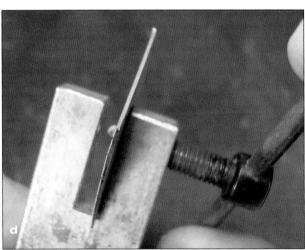

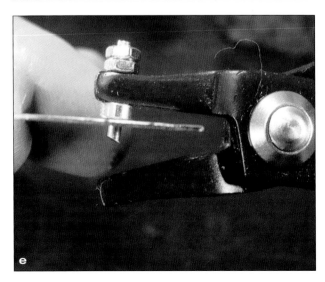

Soldering

In layman's terms, soldering means heating up one metal until it melts, introducing a second metal to the heat, mixing the two metals, and permanently bonding them together. Why does it work? At certain temperatures, the crystalline structures of metals move apart. The idea in soldering is to introduce an alloy (solder) that is fluid at exactly the same point of the maximum expansion of the metal's crystals. The alloy flows into the spaces created by the crystal expansion to create an intercrystalline bond.

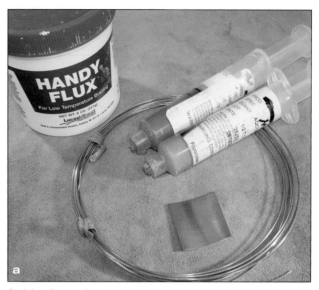

Solder

There are three types of solder available: sheet, wire, and paste **(a).** They come in four different melting temperatures: hard, medium, easy, and extra easy. Each solder flows at a different temperature—hard flows at the highest temperature and extra easy flows at the lowest temperature. When you are working on a piece with more than one join, you need a cooler melting point for each subsequent join. That way, you can work on a new join without undoing previous joins. There are several soldering methods including chip (pallion), sweat, pick, paste, and wire. The projects in this book use paste and sheet solder and both pick and sweat methods.

Flux

When heat and copper unite they create oxides. Because sterling silver is 92.5 percent silver mixed with 7.5 percent copper, you must use flux to keep silver clean. Without flux, the solder cannot stick. The flux absorbs oxygen, prevents it from combining with the copper, and primes the silver so the solder can flow. If you are using silver solder sheet or wire, you must apply flux prior to soldering. Silver solder paste has the flux built in.

Pickle

Pickle is a chemical bath that removes oxides and flux residue from metal. One type of pickle is branded Sparex. It is sodium bisulfate. If it is not convenient for you to purchase Sparex from a jewelry supplier, you can use a pool product called Ph Decreaser or Ph Down. Pickle should be used warm, but not at a boil. The fumes can be dangerous if it is heated too high. A small crock pot is the best way to heat pickle at your soldering station. Remember to always put the water in the crock pot first. Use standard safety procedures—be careful. Pickle has a life span. Its job is to remove oxides from metal. There are a few ways to tell if your pickle is saturated: It might take longer to remove oxides, or it turns blue **(b)**. If either happens to your pickle, put your pot in a sink and neutralize the pickle with baking soda **(c)**. It will do the old "volcano" trick, so put it in the sink before neutralizing. Once the frothing is done, the acid is neutralized, and it is safe to flush the pickle down the drain.

Solder board

There are many different types of solder boards and many opinions about what's best to use. I prefer a Solderite board for solder paste and a fire brick for solder sheet. A Solderite board does not retain heat. This is important when using paste because the flux is built in. If you place your item to be soldered on a hot board, the flux will begin to melt and your solder will not stay where you need it. On the other hand, a fire brick does retain heat, so it helps bring your metal up to temperature when you're using sheet solder so that it flows more quickly.

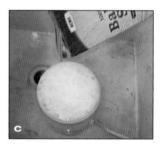

Torch

What is the best torch? It's a complicated answer because, once again, opinions vary. What it comes down to is: You need the torch that you are comfortable with and that gets the job done. Torches are described by the kind of fuel they use: butane **(d)**, propane **(e)**, MAPP gas **(f)** and acetylene **(g)**. Many beginners are comfortable with a butane torch because these small, handheld torches can be used in the kitchen. The tiny torches made for culinary use don't get hot enough for soldering, however; for jewelry making, get a "pro" version that heats to at least 2400°F, like the Blazer or the Wall Lenk LPT-500.

A common torch used in lapidary or jewelry schools is an acetylene/air torch—an acetylene tank with a handle that infuses oxygen. It has different tips for flames of different sizes. There are a variety of handles available. The Prestalite, Uniweld, and

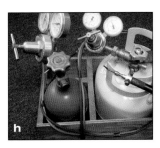

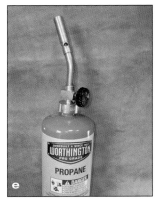

Goss are interchangeable. The Smith will only use Smith parts. Other torches require an oxygen/fuel mix. You can choose between acetylene or propane. Propane burns more cleanly.

A popular torch among bench jewelers is the Smith Little Torch **(h)**. It's a propane/oxygen torch with a very hot, small flame. When using any fuel/oxygen torch, you must adjust the gas and the oxygen for the flame you desire. Use this acronym to remember how to turn the torch on and off: POOP—Propane on/Oxygen on, Oxygen off/Propane off. For any torch without an automatic igniter you'll need a striker. It is the striker and the "pop" of the torch that frighten most new students. Battery-operated strikers work very well for those who don't like the manual sort. Never use a lighter to light a torch; it's a serious fire hazard. If you don't have a striker, use a match. Secure your torch to a pole or in a cart so it can't be knocked over. Work in a well-ventilated space and have a large fire extinguisher handy. Purchase fire extinguishers at a home supply store.

It takes some practice to get comfortable with the torch. Don't expect too much too fast. Practice makes perfect.

For the projects in this book, I use an acetylene B setup and a Smith Little Torch.

Basic soldering using solder paste

- basic soldering tool kit
- item to be soldered

1. Align the metals. A tightly fitting connection is very important. Solder does not fill holes, so the metals must touch. If the metals overlap, they will solder that way, so take your time and get your metals lined up right. Apply 2 mm balls of solder paste to the metal to be joined, spaced evenly **(a)**.

2. Begin warming up by gently and slowly moving the flame around the edge of the metals. If you have several pieces, remember to heat the bigger metals first. Watch for the metals to begin to change colors. This is a sign that they're heating up. Continue to move the flame **(b)**.

3. Bring the torch flame to the solder. Do not pull away when the solder flames up, this is just the alcohol in the flux burning off. Continue to move the flame over the solder **(c)**.

4. When the flux flame dies down, continue to move your torch flame evenly over the join. You should see the flow within 30 seconds. Flow is the term used when the solder alloy liquefies. It looks like mercury from an old-time thermometer **(d)**.

5. Let the solder cool a few seconds, then flip the piece over and make the solder flow once more to even out **(e)**.

6. Remove the flame and let the metals cool.

7. Pickle. Remove from the pickle with copper tongs and rinse.

8. When you bring the soldered piece out of the pickle, it is not going to look shiny. The metal will have a matte appearance. This is a result of the heating. You have shocked the crystal structure of the metal and it is standing on end, like bed head. Once you buff the silver with a brass brush, it will shine again.

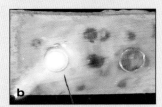

Basic soldering using chip solder

- soldering tool kit
- item to be soldered

1. Cut the solder into small chips **(a–c)**.

2. Paint flux on the metal at the join **(d, e)**.

3. Place one solder chip on the dominant-hand side of your solder board. Apply heat to the chip until it balls up **(f)**.

4. Use a pick to scoop up the solder ball **(g)**.

5. Apply heat to the join.

6. Place the balled solder on the join and continue heating evenly until it flows **(h)**.

7. Remove the heat, and let the metal cool.

8. Pickle, rinse, and brass brush.

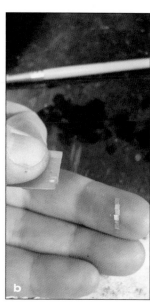

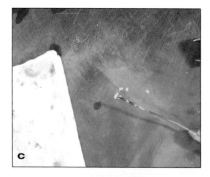

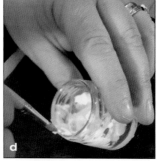

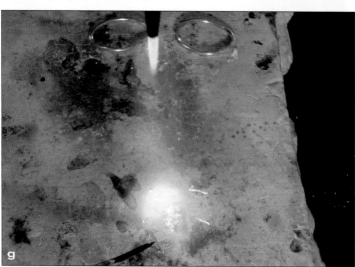

Foldforming

Foldforming was developed by Charles Lewton-Brain. It is a forging technique, but it can also be used to texture.

Line fold

1. Anneal a piece of 24-gauge metal **(a)** (see page 28 for annealing instructions).
2. Fold the metal where you would like your first line to be, and flatten with a hammer **(b)**.
3. Anneal the metal and open with an oyster or butter knife **(c, d)**.
4. Make more folds by repeating these steps as many times as desired **(e)**.
5. When you have made the desired number of folds, pickle, rinse, and brass brush.

TIP Hammering an edge all the way down or running folded metal through a rolling mill makes a very tight fold. Leaving the fold loose makes a large lazy fold. Both can be aesthetically pleaseing, depending on your design.

Leaf fold

1. Anneal a piece of 24-gauge metal and fold it in half **(f)**.
2. Make a mark ¼ in. from the fold on both ends **(g)**.
3. Use shears or a jeweler's saw and cut an arch from the mark up to the center and back down to the mark at the opposite fold.
4. Using a bordering hammer, begin hammering from the center of the cut edge in close strikes, moving down the curve to the mark. Repeat to texture toward the other mark **(h)**.

Flip the metal over and repeat on the other side **(i)**.
5. Anneal the metal and repeat these steps until you are happy with the shape.
6. Anneal the metal and open with the blunt knife **(j)**.
7. Pickle, rinse, and brass brush.

Pod fold (reverse ruffle fold)

To make a pod fold, follow the instructions as for the leaf fold, except in Step 5 hammer on the fold instead of on the cut.

Nautilus fold (forged line fold)

1. Anneal a piece of 24-gauge metal.
2. Fold the metal in half.
3. Using a cross peen hammer, begin hammering from the center of the folded edge in close strikes, moving to the end **(k)**.
4. Flip the piece of metal over and repeat on the other side.
5. Anneal the metal and repeat until you are happy with the shape.
6. Anneal the metal and open with a dull knife **(l)**.
7. Pickle, rinse, and brass brush.

There are many other wonderful folding techniques in Charles Lewton-Brain's book, *Foldforming*. I highly recommend this book. It's one of my favorites.

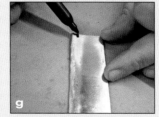

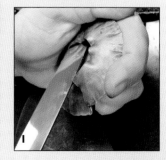

Finishing

There are many ways to finish metal. Filing smooths edges and prevents snags. Work-hardening keeps the final shape intact. Dapping creates dimensional shape. Texturing and etching create patterns, while patina adds color. Tumbling gives a final polish as well as hardens the finished piece.

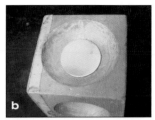

Filing

Files take the rough edges away. Always file in one direction, and support the piece while filing **(a)**. A bench pin is a good support. If you don't have a bench pin, use a scrap piece of 2 x 3-in. wood or a rubber block. If your hand cramps easily or it is difficult for you to grasp small parts, use a ring clamp to help hold the piece **(b)**. Move the file in long, graceful strokes away from your body along the edge of the metal. You will find that you don't have to work nearly as hard or as long when you file this way.

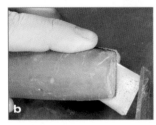

Work-hardening and annealing

Think of your metal as a container. Inside the container is a very organized crystalline structure. When you hammer, bend, or fold

metal, the crystalline structure breaks down and becomes disorganized. The crystals become smaller and smaller, compacting within the metal. Once they can break down no more, the metal becomes hard and brittle. This process is called work-hardening. After a metal is work-hardened, applying heat (annealing) causes the crystalline structure to become organized once more, and the metal is malleable.

TIP Think of your metal as a perfectly packed suitcase where everything fits and it's easy to close. When your vacation is over, you stuff all of your dirty laundry in the suitcase and suddenly it feels much fuller and it's difficult to close. When the suitcase was packed with folded, clean clothes it is like soft metal. When the suitcase is filled with rumpled dirty clothes, it is like hardened metal. When you launder, fold, and repack the suitcase, it returns to its soft state. This is a pretty good analogy for work hardening and annealing.

The best torches for annealing are propane, acetylene, or MAPP gas. You need a safe work surface such as an annealing pan filled with pumice. Use a big bushy flame on your torch and for most metals,

heat until you see a dull red. Quench as soon as the red disappears and pickle to remove the oxides. Now the metal is soft and can once again be worked. Copper, silver, nickel, gold, and brass can all be annealed this way, depending on their particular melting temperatures.

Dapping basics

The size and shape of the dapping block you use **(a)** depends on the project you are working on. The technique, however, remains the same. Wooden dapping sets are less expensive but the metal can stick in them and damage the block. If you are dapping textured metal, you are more likely to preserve the texture with a wooden dapping block. Make sure there are no burs on your disks—they will damage the block. Choose a hole on the dapping block that is much larger than the disk you are dapping **(b)**.

If you begin in a hole that is the same size or smaller than the disk, your disk will crease or fold. Choose a dap that fits in the hole and can be moved in a circular motion around the outer edge of the disk, sort of like using a mortar and pestle **(c)**. Gently tap the top of the dap with a hammer or a weighted rawhide mallet. Move the dap in concentric circles as you tap, ending in the center of the disk **(d)**.

TIP Dome a weighted raw-hide hammer by sanding one end. If you use a domed hammer, you don't need a dap.

Move the disk to smaller and smaller holes until you have the dome that you want **(e, f)**.

Texturing

While this topic could be a book in itself, I'd like to briefly explain the methods we'll be using: stamps, hammers, a rolling mill, and pure creativity.

Decorative texture and letter stamps are used in exactly the same way. They add detail or words or phrases to alter the metal surface **(a)**. Since stamping words is a little more complicated, I'll use letter stamps as my example.

Tools
- letter stamps
- 8 oz. ball-peen hammer
- bench block
- ruler
- paper and pencil

Materials
- any sheet metal

TIP: Some letter stamps have a notch indicating how it should be held. If yours don't, mark the side of each stamp that should be facing you as you strike it. Holding the stamp in the wrong position means sideways or upside-down letters.

1. Write the word or phrase you are going to stamp into the metal on a piece of paper. Count the letters and spaces. Divide the total in half to determine the center. Note the center of the phrase, and mark the center of the metal **(b)**.
2. Place the stamp of the letter that is in the middle of your word on the mark. Hold the stamp firmly in your non-dominant hand. Support the entire stamp with all four fingers on one side and your thumb on the other so that the stamp does not wiggle.
3. Hold the hammer in your dominant hand toward the end. (Choking up on the handle makes it more likely that you will hit your fingers.)
4. Rock the stamp back and forth until you feel it make total contact on the metal. When you feel the stamp resting flat on the metal, give the stamp a firm strike with the hammer **(c)**. One steady blow is all you need. If you strike the stamp more than once, you are likely to get a shadow impression
5. Finish the letters to the left of the line, and then stamp the letters to the right of the line.
6. To bring out the detail of the letters, apply patina following the basic patina instructions.

Texture hammers are a simple and effective way to add texture to your metals. Simply strike the metal in the spots in which you want to alter the surface. While there are many commercially available textures **(d)**, don't overlook flea markets and antique shops. Old hammers often have very interesting textures on them due to their years in service at their intended purpose. I prefer this type of

texture hammer in my designs because the textures are unique.

A *rolling mill* is another way to texture your metal. Use commercial texture plates, found object textures, or texture plates you make yourself by etching **(a, p. 30)**.

Tools
- rolling mill
- pattern sheets
- found texture such as lace, burlap, cheese cloth, leaves, binding wire, etc.
- cardstock

Materials
- annealed sheet metal

1. Anneal the metal before you use the rolling mill. It is not necessary to pickle the metal after annealing, but it must be very dry before rolling to avoid rust. If you are using a texture material that is hard, use a protective sheet of brass metal between the object and the sheet being textured. For instance, if you are using a piece of screen to texture a copper sheet, put the screen between the

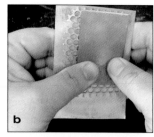

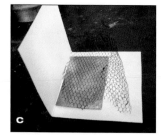

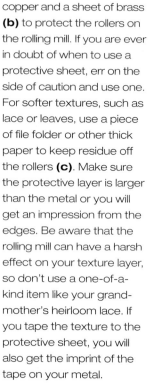

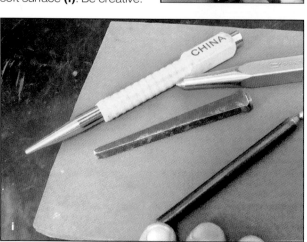

copper and a sheet of brass **(b)** to protect the rollers on the rolling mill. If you are ever in doubt of when to use a protective sheet, err on the side of caution and use one. For softer textures, such as lace or leaves, use a piece of file folder or other thick paper to keep residue off the rollers **(c)**. Make sure the protective layer is larger than the metal or you will get an impression from the edges. Be aware that the rolling mill can have a harsh effect on your texture layer, so don't use a one-of-a-kind item like your grandmother's heirloom lace. If you tape the texture to the protective sheet, you will also get the imprint of the tape on your metal.

2. For level rolling, zero the rollers. Do this by cranking them all the way down until they touch each other. If you see no light between the rollers, your rollers are at zero **(d)**.

3. Loosen the rollers so that all of the layers of metal gently slide in and out **(e)**.

4. Gradually tighten the rollers until you feel some tension as you try to

remove the layers **(f)**.

5. When you can just barely fit the layers in between the rollers, tighten the rollers by a quarter turn. The key to successfully using a rolling mill is repetitive passes, not hard passes. If you can barely crank the rollers, it is too tight. Back up and loosen the knob **(g)**. You should feel some resistance, but you should not need to grit your teeth and have a buddy help you turn the crank **(h)**.

6. Pass the layers through the crank. Remove from the back and give the knob another quarter turn.(Option: Sometimes I don't pass the layers of metal all the way out, I stop just as the end is at the back of the rollers, give the knob another quarter turn, and run the metals back through in the opposite direction. This counts as two passes. This comes in handy if you're afraid your layers will shift.)

7. Continue making passes through the rollers until you are satisfied with the results.

The rolling mill can be used for other things, too. Use it

to create other surface textures such as chip granulation and fusing . Use it in foldforming, making your own wire or sheet out of ingots, and much more. If you have access to a rolling mill, give it a try—it's a load of fun.

Creative texturing is my personal favorite. I like to use different types of tools to stamp with on varying surfaces. Use items such as a small dap from the dapping block set on the back side of the metal on a rubber mat, a flat head screw driver on an old piece of wood, or an ice pick on a soft surface **(i)**. Be creative.

How to use a tumbler

The tumbler is a must-have tool. Use a tumbler to clean metal jewelry, work-harden jump rings, cuffs, collars, and bangles, remove what I call shrimp skin from freshly pickled metals, burnish high spots through liver of sulfur patina, and much more. This is the same tool rock hounds use to tumble stones, with one difference: For jewelry, use stainless steel shot.

There are single drum, double drum, rotating drum, vibrating, and magnetic tumblers. They range in cost from $29.00 to big bucks. I have a Lortone Double Barrel Tumbler that I paid a little less than $100.00 for. It has been a real workhorse for me. I put only one barrel at a time on the rollers (my tumbler seems to work best this way). In my experience, the single barrel tumblers bog down and have a more difficult time spinning. I have one pound of stainless steel shot in each barrel.

To use the tumbler, fill the drum with water ¼ in. above the stainless steel shot **(a)**. Put 3 or 4 drops of blue Dawn dish-washing liquid or a commercial tumbling compound in the water **(b)**. Place the jewelry in the tumbler. Push the rubber seal down into the drum **(c)**. Put the outer lid on, pushing it as far down as possible, and place the washer on top **(d)**. Screw the screw top down tightly **(e)**. Place the drum on the rollers **(f)**. (If the drum does not roll evenly, you probably have either a wet drum or wet rollers.) Tumble for at

least 15 minutes. I generally tumble for about an hour. To remove the lid, use the washer to pry beneath the lip of the lid. It will pop up easily. When you have finished with the tumbler, rinse your shot and store it in the drum with the lid loosely on top.

TIP: Run a new tumbler with shot, water, and detergent for at least one hour to season the drums before you put jewelry in it. If your tumbler begins to transfer black onto your silver, it is probably dirty. Pour flat cola ¼ in. above the level of shot. Run for 15 minutes to clean the shot. Invest in stainless steel shot, because carbon steel and steel shot rust very easily and must be stored in a special liquid solution between each use to remain clean.

Patina

To polish or patina is a question of much conversation and personal choice. I like my pieces darkened or antiqued. I share my studio with another artist who shines every finished product to a mirror finish. In this book almost all of the projects are patinated, but you should certainly do what pleases you.

Most metals react to their environment, changing their color eventually, and will continue to change over time. These changes are often a result of oxidation. In jewelry making, we add intentional patinas to gain control of color outcomes.

Methods of application include immersion, heat, random contact, fuming, and direct color. One important thing to remember in applying patina to metal is that a patina is on the surface of the metal. Patina must be sealed or it will continue to change over time.

Aging

My favorite method is warm liver of sulfur solution. It gives pieces an antiqued appearance and adds shadow and dimension to the surface. Liver of sulfur solution can create a sequence of colors before it blackens your metal, depending on its temperature, solution strength, and exposure time. Different

metals react differently as well. Liver of sulfur can be purchased in lump, liquid, or gel forms. Follow the instructions provided with the type you choose. I use the lump form. I have gotten the best results by following this recipe:

1. Put 5 or 6 pea-sized lumps of liver of sulfur in a rinsed out opaque plastic bottle, like a hydrogen peroxide bottle **(a)**.

2. Fill the bottle up to the rim with water, shake, and recap.

3. Use this solution in a 1:1 ratio with water. For example, fill a jar with ½ in. of water and combine it with ½ in. of solution.

4. Refill the hydrogen peroxide bottle with water

and recap. This produces a highly concentrated liquid form of liver of sulfur that is always ready to use. When the liquid solution becomes weak yellow color, add a few more lumps of liver of sulfur.

5. Warm the solution. I keep mine in a sealed jar on a candle warmer **(b)**.

Color

In the studio, you can somewhat control colors of metal with commercial patinas or "kitchen" patinas. Both are fun to play with. Remember to always work in a well-ventilated area.

Commercial solutions will produce blue, green, and brown patinas. I have used all of them with much

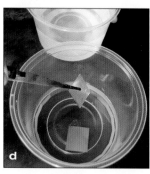

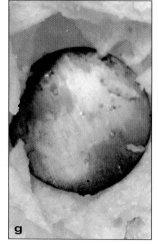

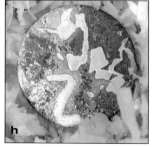

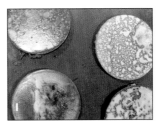

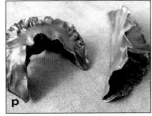

My secret formula (shh) is *white ammonia and Miracle-Gro fertilizer.* I spray it on with a spray bottle and wait about 30 minutes. It gives very quick results **(l)**.

success. Brand names include Green Midas, Green Jax, Blue Jax, and Brown Jax. Buy these solutions at most jewelry-making suppliers. For the best results, start with clean metal, use heat to remove patina, rough-up metal for better color adhesion, understand that patinas that work for copper will usually work for brass, and be patient.

For green and blue try this:
1. Scrub the metal with a coarse sanding sponge or sandpaper.
2. Wash with soap and a green kitchen scrubby until the water sheets off the metal and does not ball up.
3. Soak the metal in a saturated salt-water solution for at least 15 to 20 minutes—the longer the better, and 24 hours is the best **(c)**.

TIP To make a saturated salt-water solution, fill a container with water and add salt until the salt quits dissolving. When the salt begins to settle on the bottom of the container, you have a saturated solution, meaning the salt can dissolve no more.

4. Remove and dry the metal. Do not rinse.

5. In a disposable container with a lid, pour just enough of the commercial patina to cover the piece. These solutions usually have a strong aroma.
6. Submerge the piece in the solution and let it soak for at least 15 to 20 minutes.
7. Carefully remove the piece **(d)** and place it in a dehydrator. Move the metal to level the patina solution until there are no puddles. Check often. If you need to add color to spots where the patina did not adhere, just paint more on with a brush.
8. If you're not satisfied with the patina coating, redip the entire piece in the patina solution and put it back in the dehydrator.
9. Remove the piece, let it cool, and seal the patina onto the metal with a micro crystalline wax such as Renaissance wax or spray-on lacquer **(e)**.

Common items such as a boiled egg, salt and vinegar potato chips, cedar pet bedding, used cat litter, chewing tobacco, vinegar, salt, and ammonia can create patina. For these kitchen-chemist patinas, first follow Steps 1–4 of the commercial process. For Step 5, seal as described:

Boiled egg gives the same results as liver of sulfur. Place your piece in a sealed container with a chopped warm boiled egg **(f)**.

Bury your piece in a container filled with moistened *salt-and-vinegar potato chips* **(g)**.

Saturate *cedar pet bedding* with *white vinegar* and bury your piece in it; place in a sealed container **(h)**.

Bury your piece in a sealed container of used (yes used) *kitty litter*. Sorry you're on your own with this one.

Bury your piece in a sealed container of *vinegar- and ammonia-saturated chewing tobacco* **(i)**.

Pour ½ in. of ammonia in a sealed container. Suspend a screen over the ammonia. Set your piece on the screen and seal the container. Or, mix *salt, ammonia,* and *vinegar* together in a spray bottle. Spray the mixture on your piece. Let it dry, reapply as needed **(j)**.

Make a *liver of sulfur solution* and add *5 drops of ammonia* **(k)**.

These are all fun to experiment with, and remember, if you hate the results, heat will remove it!

Heat is a very effective way to add color. I call this method "painting with fire." The most important thing to remember is that color comes with the cool down of the metal, not the heat up, so be patient and apply and remove the heat often **(m)**. Different types of fuel give different colors as well as stages of shine on the metal. A butane torch gives slightly different colors than a propane torch, for example. On the other hand, if I have pickled and brass brushed a piece before I heat patina, I will get a shiny bright orange and pink result **(n)**. If I do not brass brush my piece and leave it in the shrimp-skin stage after firing, I will get a satin finish added to the pinks and oranges **(o)**. Often I will brass brush, liver of sulfur, sand, and then heat patina my pieces and get a deep purple and blue raku looking patina **(p)**. Sometimes you can get a beautiful red patina by bringing copper up to a glowing red heat then quenching very quickly in ice cold water. Experiment. It's fun!

Etching copper, nickel, and brass

While there aren't any etched projects in this book, it is a useful skill to learn. You can etch brass to create texture templates and use them in place of a rolling mill, for example. Ferric chloride is used for etching. It's a common solution used in the computer industry to etch computer circuit boards. You need to follow basic safety rules, such as working in a well-ventilated area, keeping the chemical off your skin, and using caution. Purchase ferric chloride online, at computer hobby shops, and at jewelry-making suppliers.

Materials

- A low-edged glass or plastic container
- Ferric chloride
- Copper, nickel, or brass sheet
- Water
- Soap
- Resist (Stayz On Ink with rubber stamps, stickers, paint pen, permanent marker, wax, or PNP Blue Paper)
- Packing tape
- Baking soda
- Green kitchen scrubbies
- Coarse sanding sponge
- 0000 steel wool
- An apron (ferric chloride stains)

The gauge of metal you choose to work with is up to you. The thing to remember is that the metal is going to become thinner during the etching process. I usually use 24-gauge sheet or thicker depending on what my final design is going to be. If I'm making a pendant, I use 24-gauge. If I'm making a pattern sheet to be used in the rolling mill or with some sort of clay, I etch 20-gauge brass so that I can etch a deeper impression.

1. Sand the sheet with a coarse grit sanding sponge to give the metal a good tooth.

2. Scrub the metal at the sink with soap and water using a green kitchen scrubby. Take care not to touch the surface you have just cleaned. Continue to scrub until you've removed all the oils, dirt, and fingerprints that could be on the surface. To test that your metal is clean enough, you should see the water run off the metal in sheets rather than bead up on the surface.

3. Apply the resist material and let it dry **(a, b)**. I do not put any kind of resist on my edges—I like the sort of reticulated look the metal

gets giving me an interesting border. If you want a clean edge, apply resist around the edges.

4. Cut a piece of packing tape 4 in. longer than your container is wide and deep. Tape the back of your metal to the center of this piece of tape **(c)**.

5. Fill the container with ¼ in. of ferric chloride. Attach 2 in. of tape to one side of the container **(d)**.

6. Suspend the metal face down in the ferric chloride. Allow the metal to sit just on top of the solution. If you lower one end in and then gently lower the rest down you will not get any air bubbles **(e)**. Attach the other side of the tape to the opposite side of the container. Write the time on the end of the tape.

7. Set a timer for one hour. If you have a way to agitate the container you will get a better etching. (See page 12 for agitation tips.)

8. After one hour, lift one end of the tape. Using a tooth pick or chop stick or something disposable, run down the surface being etched to feel for ridges. The resist may fool you into thinking that the metal has

etched, when actually all you are seeing is the ink **(f)**. If you are satisfied with how deep the etch feels, then remove the tape trapeze from the etching solution and deposit it into a bowl with a water/baking soda mix in it. This will neutralize the ferric chloride **(g)**.

9. Remove the tape and rinse the metal in water. Scrub the remaining ferric chloride off of the metal with the green kitchen scrubby. Rinse and dry the metal.

10. Sand the metal with a coarse sanding sponge. Wear a mask when sanding the ferric chloride from the metal.

11. The ferric chloride can be used again, but it will not be as strong as the first time it was used, and each time it is used it becomes weaker and requires much longer etching times. Once the ferric chloride is saturated, neutralize it with baking soda **(h)** and dispose of it. Neutralized ferric chloride is supposedly safe enough to flush, but it is better to store it until you can get it to your local fire department or recycling center.

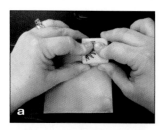

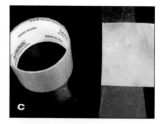
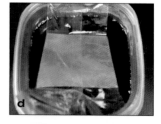

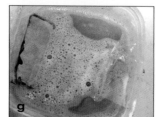

Making Findings

Findings—should you buy them or make them? Yes! You heard me. You should make them, and you should buy them. Sometimes it just makes sense to use a purchased finding. Yes, you could make all of your findings, but then again, you could reinvent the wheel every time you go for a drive, too. Handmade findings have their appeal, but sometimes a pre-made finding just goes better with the finished piece, just saves time. The key is using the right findings. Use only quality pre-made findings. Don't scrimp. Also, stay within the design of your piece. If you've made an organic looking pendant, don't put a high-polish lobster-claw clasp on it when a simple S-hook would fit the design much better. Here are my favorite handmade findings.

Make a headpin (drawing a bead on the end of a wire)

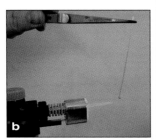

Tools
- torch
- tweezers
- pickle
- quench pot
- copper tongs
- brass brush
- sanding sponge

Materials
- copper, silver, or gold wire

1. Using tweezers, hold a piece of wire in the flame of a torch at the point where the flame turns from blue to orange **(a)**.
2. Flash the wire up and down in flame to heat the entire piece of wire.
3. Concentrate the heat on the tip of the wire. Keep the flame steady on the tip until the end begins to ball **(b)**.
4. Let the wire cool, pickle, rinse, and brass brush. (Option: you can simply sand the firescale off of the wire with a coarse sanding sponge.)
5. If the ball has dimples and you want to remove these use a file. (Option: Use fine silver instead of sterling silver and you will not get firescale or dimples in your drawn bead.)

Making earring wires

1. Cut two 2½-in. pieces of 20-gauge wire.
2. Draw a bead on the wire ends as in making a headpin. Remove any fire scale.
3. Working with both wires at a time, place roundnose pliers against the balls **(a)**.
4. Bend the wires all the way around the roundnose pliers until they touch the balls again **(b)**.
5. Hold a permanent marker in your non-dominant hand, place the loops against the seam of the cap, and hold in place with your thumb **(c)**. Bend the wires all the way around the pen until the wires touch the loops **(d)**.
6. Place the edge of an earring wire on an anvil or bench block. Flare the edge slightly with a hammer **(e)**. Repeat with the second wire.
7. Hammer to work-harden using a soft blow hammer on a soft surface.
8. Round the ends with a file or wire rounding cup bur.

Jump rings

Making your own jump rings means you can tailor gauge and size to any project. You have several tool options: Try a wrap-n-tap tool **(a)**, wooden dowel, or a carpenter's pencil **(b)**. Saw your jump rings apart **(c)**, or use flush cutters and cut each jump ring individually **(d)**.

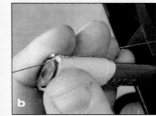

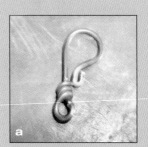

Clasps If you have wire or sheet metal, you can make your own clasps.

Clasps can be made by soldering or by using cold connections **(a)**.

Kim's Tips

These are some—definitely not all—of my little tips. Use them as you will and enjoy.

Closing a large hole

If your rivet hole is too large, gently tap the hole with a ball-peen hammer or a dap.

Curing burns

Rinse a burn in cold water. Sprinkle with baking soda and rinse again. Spray with Sovereign Silver Gel. The burn goes away and there is no pain! Love it! Keep it in your tool box.

Propping for soldering

Not only is binding wire great for jewelry making, it's also a great tool. During soldering, you may need to prop or bind your piece on a piece of wire "furniture."

Adjusting stone height

Use polymer clay to raise stones to the proper height in bezels.

Cleaning a solder board

Rub the board on pavement to remove flux and solder.

Flush cutting jump rings

Use metal shears to flush cut larger jump rings.

Tightening a loose hammer head

Soak overnight in anti-freeze to swell wood handles and tighten the hammer heads.

Leveling a dome

Mark the edge of a domed disk with a permanent marker. Sand the disk until the marker is gone. The dome is level.

Annealing sterling silver

Use a permanent marker to mark the silver. While you're annealing the metal, the ink will disappear. Once it's gone, the metal is annealed.

Straightening or work-hardening wire

Roll the wire between two bench blocks or anvils.

Flattening metal

Whack your metal between two bench blocks or anvils.

Controlling the viscosity of solder paste

Add enough water to solder paste so it is the consistency of pancake batter.

Equal sizing

If one piece of metal is larger than another but they should match, place them together, trace the overlap with a permanent marker, and file away the marked sections.

Polishing

After soldering or annealing, metal looks dull and has a frosty or satin finish. Use a brass brush, buffing wheel, or tumbler to return the metal to its familiar shiny self.

Finding the center

Use a round needlepoint mat to locate the center of a round disk.

Saving silver ruined by compromised pickle

Oh no! Someone put tweezers in the pickle pot and now the silver is pink. No worries. Make a solution of one part pickle and one part hydrogen peroxide. Put the piece in the solution and watch the pink disappear.

(Don't leave it in too long, or the piece will disappear too.) Neutralize the peroxide–pickle solution with baking soda when you are finished and dispose of it properly.

Soldering copper

There is no copper-colored solder. Use silver solder and place steel binding wire in the pickle pot with the piece to copperplate the silver solder.

Resurrecting compromised pickle

Remove the ferrous metal from the pickle, and it is no longer compromised.

Sizing roofing copper

Roofing copper is not sold by gauge. If you want 24-gauge copper, ask for 16-oz. or .021 in. copper.

Extending the lifespan of flux

Put a little flux in a small sealable container like a film canister or a single-serving jelly jar from a restaurant. You won't introduce contaminants from your flux brush to your full container of flux.

Chapter 1

The projects in this chapter are designed to introduce you to your hands. You must reacquaint yourself with your hands in order to be perfectly accustomed to holding and working with tools. This may sound peculiar to you, but it is quite serious. Tools must become an extension of your hands: Become one with your tools.

These projects are simple. Each introduces you to a tool set, and asks you to manipulate the tools to accomplish a goal. The three primary cold connection or metal forging tools used here are the anvil, the hammer, and the saw or metal shears. Before you begin, practice loading a jewelers saw, using a domed chasing hammer to smooth out metal, and swinging a hammer. Become comfortable with allowing the hammer to do the work, not you.

Think of these exercises as a dress rehearsal before starting the actual project:

- Swing your hammer and strike a scrap block of wood repeatedly in the same spot until you can take your eyes off the spot and still strike it
- Draw zigzag and curly lines with a marker on scrap metal and then try to saw them without breaking a blade
- Experiment with your metal shears and see how small you can cut out a circle of metal— how tight can you cut?

Have fun with these projects and just remember that you are striving for tool Zen. Relax, release the tension in your muscles, and go for it.

Cigar Band Ring

This is a classic ring, and a great one! There are so many variations to such a simple ring. **You can stamp it, engrave it, leave it open and adjustable, solder it, add patina, or flare the edges.** You can't lose with this ring.

Ring size chart (24 gauge)

US SIZE	UK SIZE	RING BLANK LENGTH
5	J	50.55 mm
5½	K	51.81 mm
6	L	53.07 mm
6½	M	54.32 mm
7	N	55.58 mm
7½	O	56.83 mm
8	P	58.09 mm
8½	Q	59.35 mm
9	R	60.60 mm
9½	S	61.86 mm
10	T	63.11 mm
10½	U	64.37 mm
11	V	65.63 mm
11½	W	66.88 mm
12	X	68.14 mm
12½	Y	69.39 mm
13	Z	70.65 mm

stamping • liver of sulfur patina

Basic Tool Kits
- Texturing and letter stamping
- Patina

Tools
- Graph paper
- Pencil
- Rubber cement
- Shears
- Files
- Sanding sponge
- Ring mandrel
- Soft blow hammer (rubber, rawhide, nylon)
- Large stepped pliers

Materials
- ¾-in. wide piece of 24-gauge sterling silver sheet, approximately 3 in. long, depending on the size of ring

1. Add half a size to your ring size and use the ring sizing chart to determine the required length of silver sheet. (Example: if you wear a size 7 ring, you will need a length for a 7½).

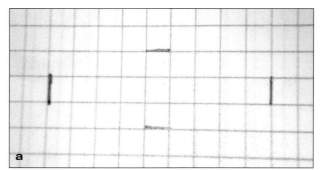

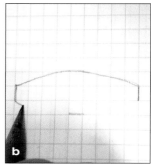

2. Draw a rectangle on the graph paper that is ¾-in. wide and the length you determined in Step 1. Mark the center of the length. At each end of the rectangle, mark the center third of the width. This needs to be reasonably correct, but you can estimate it using the graph paper instead of measuring to the nearest millimeter **(a)**. Draw a line connecting the center mark on each side to the end marks to make a ring template shaped like a cigar band **(b)**.

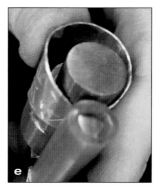

3. Cut out the template. Try the template on your finger.

4. Glue the template to the edge of the sheet metal. Using metal shears or a jeweler's saw, cut out the ring blank **(c)**. Remove the template.

5. Use a file to round the ends and a sanding sponge to round out the edges of the ring.

6. Place the ring blank on the bench block and stamp random letters on one side **(d)**. Use large stepped pliers to shape the ring **(e)**.

Alternatively, center the ring blank on a ring mandrel over the mark for the desired ring size. Use a soft blow hammer to shape the ring over the mandrel. Flip the ring on the mandrel so the ring is evenly shaped **(f)**.

7. Place the ring in a warm liver of sulfur solution, rinse, dry, and sand away excess patina with 0000 steel wool. Remove enough patina so the letters contrast with the silver **(g)**.

Twisted Paddle Earrings

This pair of earrings is a perfect "starter project" because you'll become familiar with common tools, terms, and techniques before moving on to more challenging projects. **It's a quick project: If you begin in the morning, you'll be showing off your new earrings by lunchtime.** It's also a project that gives you lots of flexibility: Substitute copper or brass wire for the sterling silver wire, change the shapes, and explore the numerous possibilities of this design.

TIP: Use almost any shape for this project. Mix it up!

cold connections • liver of sulfur patina • making earring wires

Tool Kits
- Cold connection
- Patina
- Wirewrapping

Materials
- 2-in. square of 24-gauge copper sheet, depending on your design
- 4 in. 14-gauge sterling silver wire
- **2** #2 size iron carpet tacks (or another rivet style)
- 8 in. 26-gauge sterling silver wire
- pair of earring wires (page 23)

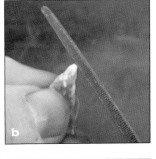

1. Cut out two ¾ x ¾-in. squares and two triangles of similar size from the copper sheet. Texture all the copper pieces **(a)**.

2. Use a file to remove the sharp corners, then use a coarse sanding sponge to smooth all the edges of the textured copper **(b, c)**.

3. Cut two 2-in. pieces of 14-gauge sterling silver wire. Using a chasing hammer, paddle both ends of both pieces of wire on a bench block or anvil. Make sure the paddles will accommodate a ¹⁄₁₆-in. hole **(d)**.

4. Use roundnose pliers to make a loop in the center of each 14-gauge paddled wire **(e)**.

5. Position a paddle on a copper square and triangle

(f). Use a spring-loaded punch to dimple holes in the copper and silver pieces **(g)**.

6. Drill ¹⁄₁₆-in. holes in each of the dimples.

7. Insert an iron carpet tack (or other rivet material) in the top hole of the silver paddle and the bottom hole of the top piece of copper. Flip the piece over and use "sacrificial cutters" to trim the end of the tack 1 mm above the copper **(h, i)**. File the tack to remove any burs.

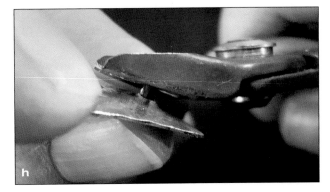

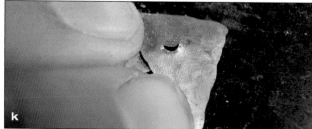

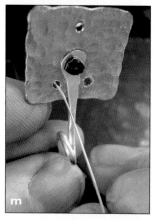

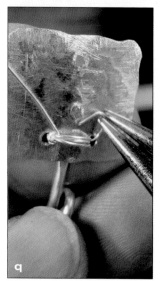

8. Position the silver loop over the edge of the anvil so you can flare your rivet on a flat surface. Using the flat face of the hammer, flare the tack out over the copper **(j, k)**. Use the rounded end of the hammer to flatten down the rivet edges. Repeat to flare the second rivet.

9. Use a spring-loaded punch to make a dimple in the square piece of copper on each side of the silver paddle just below the iron rivet **(l)**. Drill a 1/16-in. hole in

each dimple to create lashing holes.

10. Cut a 4-in. piece of 26-gauge sterling silver wire. Thread one end of the wire into one of the holes in the copper **(m)**. Leave a 1/4-in. tail, and begin lashing the wire around the silver paddle and the copper **(n)**. When the holes are filled (four to five loops around), thread the end of the lashing wire through the loop formed in the back of the copper piece twice. Push the loops down to the copper as close as possible, and trim the excess wire **(o, p)**.

11. Loop the 1/4-in. tail through the loop one time and trim **(q)**.

12. Repeat Steps 5–11 to make a second earring.

13. Patina the earrings in liver of sulfur solution. Rinse and dry. Use 0000 steel wool to remove excess patina allowing the silver to shine and show off the texture of the copper.

14. Add your own earring wires (or use a purchased pair) using the holes at the top of the earrings.

A Little Bit Whompy Stack Ring

Here's a popular project that's always a little different every time it's made. This ring has seen many changes. I have used wooden bases and metal bases, lampworked beads, stones, buttons and anything flat. **I call this ring my "attitude ring" 'cause you gotta have lots of moxie to carry it off.** In some states I think you may have to register it as a lethal weapon.

cold connections • liver of sulfur patina • forming

Tool Kits
- Cold connection
- Patina
- Texturing

Tools
- Large stepped pliers
- Two-hole punch
- Ring mandrel
- Rolling mill (optional)

Materials
- 3 x ½-in. piece of 24-gauge copper sheet
- **1–4** flat beads, with ¹⁄₁₆-in. holes to make a ¼-in. stack (These lampworked beads are made by the very talented JoAnne Zekowski)
- 1-in. .080 micro screw with nut
- **2** 2 x 3 mm tube rivets or sterling silver tube crimps

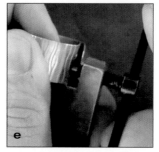

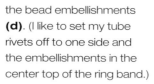

TIP: This is a great project for rolling mill texture.

1. Cut a ½-in. wide strip of copper that is ½ in. longer than the length of metal needed for your desired ring size. (For example, a size 7 ring = 2¼ in. + ½ in.= the length of metal needed for the ring band.) Texture, round the ends, and file the edges of the band **(a)**.

2. Use large stepped pliers to form the strip into a ring **(b)**. Overlap the ends by ¼ in. **(c)**.

3. Place the band on a metal ring mandrel and use a spring-loaded punch to make two dimples in the band for rivet holes, and one hole in the center for

the bead embellishments **(d)**. (I like to set my tube rivets off to one side and the embellishments in the center top of the ring band.)

4. Open the band and using the two-hole punch, make two ⁹⁄₃₂-in. holes in the band for the tube rivets. Make both holes in the top of the band and only one in the lower lip of the band. If you make all four holes, they may not line up after the first rivet because the rivet can often put the metal in a bind **(e, f)**.

5. Make one ¹⁄₁₆-in. hole in the center for the bead embellishments.

6. Place a tube (crimp) on a bench block and gently flair one side with a center punch **(g, h)**. Reshape the band, thread the 1-in. screw in the center hole for your embellishments **(i)**, and insert one of the flared tube rivets in one of the attachment holes.

TIP: Placing the screw before you rivet the band together is easier, especially with a small ring.

7. Place the band back on the metal ring mandrel **(j)**. Using the center punch again, gently flair the other side of the tube rivet **(k)**. Continue flaring the tube rivet with a small hammer.

8. Use the two-hole punch and the hole already drilled in the top of the ring to make the second hole. Set the second tube rivet in the band using the same method as the previous tube rivet **(l)**.

9. Now that the band is complete, design the rest of the ring. This can be elaborate or simple, depending on your taste. You can combine found objects with lampworked beads and other metal pieces. The choices are limitless. If you are using metal components and you are planning on a liver of sulfur patina, do so now.

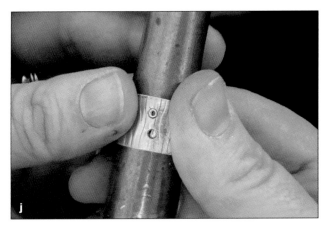

10. Make sure the embellishments have ¹⁄₁₆ in. or larger holes in them. Begin stacking embellishments on the screw extending from the top of the band **(m)**. When you have all of your "doodads" in place, screw on the nut. Place a fingertip over the screw head and tighten the nut with a pair of chainnose pliers **(n)**.

Trim the end of the screw 1 mm above the nut. Place the ring back on the metal ring mandrel and gently file and flare out the end of the screw over the nut **(o)**.

Forged African-inspired Ring

My friend brought me a ring like this and asked, "Do you think you can make one?" **I took it in my hands, checked the twist of the wires, and replied, "Piece of cake."** I messed up my first piece of 11-gauge sterling silver...ouch!, by forgetting one very basic rule of forging metals: Once metal is flattened, it will only bend forward and backwards, not in a downward arch. So I put that silver in the scrap box, backed up, punted, and tried again. Now I know to bend the wire in an arch before I hammer it! Duh!

forging • stamping • liver of sulfur patina

Tool Kits
- Texturing
- Patina

Tools
- Domed chasing hammer
- Anvil or bench block
- Files
- Ring mandrel
- Flex shaft with brown Cratex wheel
- Soft blow hammer (rubber, rawhide, nylon)
- Pencil
- Ruler

Materials
- 5½ in. 11-gauge sterling silver wire, depending on the size ring you are making

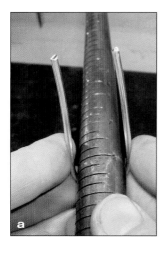

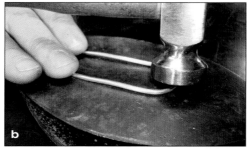

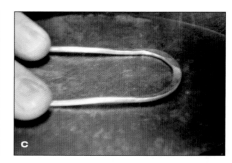

1. Use the ring chart (page 38) to determine the length of wire needed to make your ring, add 2½ in., and cut the wire.

2. Mark the wire in the center and ½ in. on each side of center. (The two outer marks show the center inch of the wire). Because forging the center of the wire will harden the wire so that it will not easily bend, form the center section of the ring before it is forged.

3. Center the wire on the ring mandrel. Curve the ends of the wire to make a large U-shape with the center inch of the wire in the center of the U. Shape with a soft blow hammer **(a)**.

4. With a domed chasing hammer and bench block, flare out the wire starting at the center mark **(b)**. Continue flaring and flattening the marked 1-in. section of wire, making the center the widest flared section. Your goal is a ¼-in. arch at its highest point **(c)**. The arch should have a smooth edge, not jagged or textured.

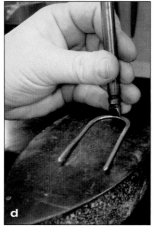

5. Use texture stamps to adorn one or both sides of the arch **(d)**.

TIP: Remember, less texture can be more.

6. Position the forged arch section of the wire on the ring mandrel at your desired size mark, and pull the two ends of the wire up and over the ring mandrel **(e)**.

7. Use a soft blow hammer to shape and work-harden the ring **(f)**.

8. Use a flex shaft with a brown Cratex wheel to smooth the ends of the wire to a gradual rounded point. Not too much work is needed, just enough so

that the wires have a nice gradual taper **(g)**.

9. Place the ring in a warm liver of sulfur solution, rinse, dry, and remove excess patina with 0000 steel wool. Remove enough patina so that the stamped texture contrasts with the silver finish.

Scarf Pin

During a weeklong workshop, one of my students was knitting a beautiful scarf in the evenings after class. When she finished, she brought it to show me. It happened to be the day we were doing foldforming. After we did the line fold segment of the class she had the scarf and the folded copper both sitting on her workbench. **The two pieces looked so good together, I suggested she make a scarf pin out of the copper.** Needless to say, by the end of the day we all had foldformed scarf pins. One student with lovely long thick hair pulled her hair back with it as a barrette. Two for one: If you get warm, take off your scarf and pull back your hair.

foldforming • liver of sulfer patina • dapping • adding texture • disk cutting

Tool Kits
- Foldforming
- Texturing
- Patina
- Annealing

Tools
- Disk cutter
- Rounded hammer or dresser knob
- Large wooden dapping block

Materials
- 3 x 3-in. piece of 24-gauge copper
- 6-in. piece of 6-gauge copper grounding wire
- Renaissance wax or acrylic sealer

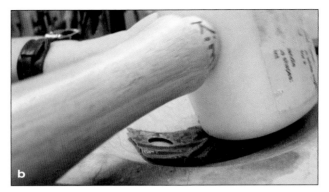

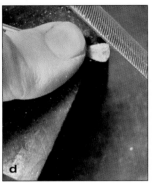

1. Make a line fold with the 3 x 3 in. piece of copper sheet (page 27).

2. Use a disk cutter to cut two holes on opposite sides of the copper sheet **(a)**. File all the edges.

3. Place the copper sheet in a large wooden dapping block and dap it slightly using a rounded hammer or dresser knob **(b)**.

4. Anneal the piece of 6-gauge wire and paddle the end **(c)**. File the ends round **(d)** and curve into a loop **(e, f)**.

5. Insert the stick in one hole and out the other. Trim the end to about 1 in. **(g)**. Remove the stick and file the end to a point **(h)**.

6. Apply liver of sulfer or heat to patinate the copper and the pin. The piece in this picture was heat patinated and the stick was put in liver of sulfur.

7. Seal with Renaissance wax or acrylic spray.

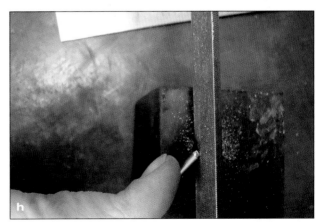

Copper Collar

I am very impatient when it comes to making chain. It's time consuming and I become bored with the repetitive patterns. It's so bad that I even stooped so low as to sign my poor husband up for a chain mail workshop without telling him, hoping that he would start making my chains for me, but no such luck. He loved the class, and is very good at chain making, but I still can't get him to make mine for me. This collar is quick and easy. I like that.

rolling mill • annealing • hand forming

TIP: Do not pickle before using the rolling mill—you do not want to accidentally transfer pickle to the rollers of your rolling mill.

Tool Kits
- Annealing
- Texturing

Tools
- Rolling mill
- Files
- Bracelet-bending pliers
- Soft blow hammer
- Tumbler

Materials
- 8 in. 6-gauge copper wire
- Renaissance wax

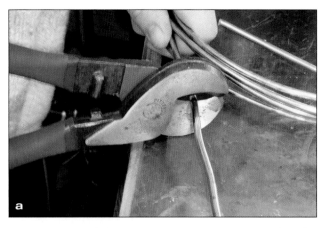

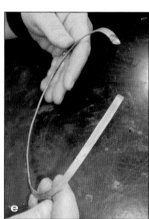

1. Cut an 8-in. piece of 6 gauge copper wire **(a)**.

2. Anneal **(b)**, rinse, and dry. Make sure the copper is very dry before using the rolling mill.

3. Set the rollers of the mill to 6 gauge by sliding the wire in and out of the rollers, tightening and loosening until the wire can just barely be pulled out. Tighten the rolling mill a quarter turn and run the wire through the rollers. Continue running the wire through the rolling mill, increasing the pressure by a quarter turn each pass, until the wire is 16-in. long **(c)**.

4. Fold the wire into a gentle loop so that it will fit into the annealing pan and anneal **(d)**.

5. Pickle, rinse, and brass brush.

6. Start at the center of the collar and begin to shape the collar with your hands until you are pleased with the fit **(e)**.

7. File the ends round **(f)**.

8. Use bracelet-bending pliers to make a nice curve on each end of the collar **(g)**.

9. Gently hammer with a soft blow hammer **(h)**, gently texture, if desired, or tumble (if you have a tumbler that's large enough) to work-harden the shape.

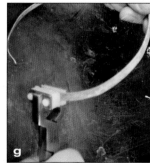

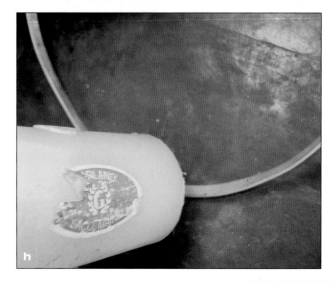

Heart Divided Pendant

I lifted this design from my friend, Margaret. She took one of my foldforming classes and came in the next day and said, **"Look what I made last night."** I asked to use it as a project in the book and there you have it. It's funny because she didn't think I'd like it because I'm not a heart person. But the fact that she used brass and that it looked great appealed to me! So she wins. I now have a heart in my book.

foldforming • line fold • annealing

Tool kits
- Annealing
- Wirewrapping
- Foldforming
- Texturing
- Patina (optional)

Tools (Pendant)
- Files and sanding sponge
- Metal shears
- Hole punch
- Bordering hammer
- Center punch

Tools (Chain)
- Heavy-duty cutters
- Medium stepped pliers
- Domed chasing hammer
- Ball-peen hammer

Materials (Pendant)
- 3 x 4-in. piece of 24-gauge brass sheet
- **2** ⅛-in. eyelets (optional)

Materials (Chain)
- 1 yd. 18-gauge steel binding wire
- Renaissance wax

1. Anneal the brass sheet **(a)** and fold in half.

2. Using metal shears, cut a half-heart shape out of the metal by cutting from the folded corner, diagonally up to the open corner, and back down to the folded corner ½ in. from the top **(b)**.

3. Lock the heart in a vise fold-side up with about ¹⁄₁₆ in. protruding. Use a texture stamp along the folded edge **(c)**.

4. Remove the brass and place it on an anvil or bench block **(d)**. Using a bordering hammer, hammer with close blows from the rounded edge to the fold **(e)** and from the curve down to the point **(f)**.

5. Remove the brass from the vise and anneal **(g)**.

6. Use an oyster knife or other dull knife to open the folded heart **(h)**. If you would like to ruffle the edges more, use the bordering hammer and hammer along the edges again **(i)**.

7. Sand the edges with a coarse sanding sponge **(j)**.

8. Make two ⅛-in. holes in the top of the heart. If desired, set eyelets in holes.

9. The annealing process should have created a very attractive patina. Use steel wool or a sanding sponge, if needed, to enhance. Do not pickle.

"S" chain

1. Cut and condition a yard of binding wire (page. 16).

2. From the prepared length, cut 12 2-in. pieces and flush cut each end with heavy-duty cutters.

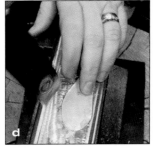

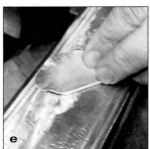

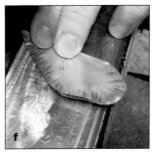

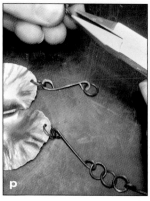

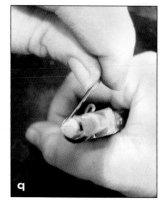

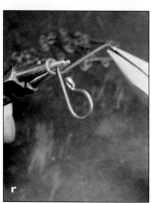

3. Using roundnose pliers, curl each end of the wire in opposite directions **(k)**.

4. Place the S link you have made on the anvil and hammer it flat with the domed chasing hammer, flaring out the loops on each end **(l)**. Use the ball-peen hammer to tap closed each loop on the link **(m)**.

5. Use the medium barrel of the medium stepped pliers to make a coil of 14 jump rings **(n)**. Use the sawing jig to cut the coil down the middle to create flush-cut jump rings **(o)**.

6. Attach jump rings and S links to create chain

(p). (Be creative with your patterns to create unique chains.) Make more links and jump rings if you want a chain longer than 17 in.

7. Cut a 3-in. piece of conditioned binding wire. Tightly curl the end with roundnose pliers.

8. Using the middle barrel of the medium stepped pliers, adjust the curl flush with the pliers. Wrap the wire around the barrel creating a miniature shepherds hook **(q)**.

9. Remove the wire and grasp it with the middle of the roundnose pliers about ¼ in. above the curve **(r)**.

10. Make a basic wrapped loop with the remaining wire **(s)** to attach the hook to the chain.

11. Hold the hook on the edge of an anvil and flatten the top of the hook with a chasing hammer.

12. Attach the hook to one end of the chain with a jump ring **(t)**.

Chapter 2

You are now acquainted with your hands, you are comfortable with the tools used in Chapter 1, and you are ready to add some more skills to your repertoire. In this chapter the tasks will push your abilities to a higher level. You'll add several new tools and techniques to the mix as well. You'll start to solder and experiment with a torch. You can use a butane torch that heats to at least 2400° F, such as the Blazer or Wall Lenk LPT-500. For the projects in this book, I use an acetylene B torch setup and a Smith Little Torch.

These projects are rewarding, but always keep in mind that projects presented to you in instructional format are meant to teach you techniques and inspire you to come up with new designs of your own based on what you've learned. For example, you may not care for the "nightmare catcher" because you don't like skulls. Well, don't discard the project! Change the interior design. Cut out a butterfly instead of a skull, or a peace sign. It's the wiring technique that is important. None of these projects is limited to the way I made it—take the techniques and design foundation, and run with it. Change from round wire to square, add a color patina, dangle crystals off the ends, take ownership of your work, ask yourself, "what if?" and then do it.

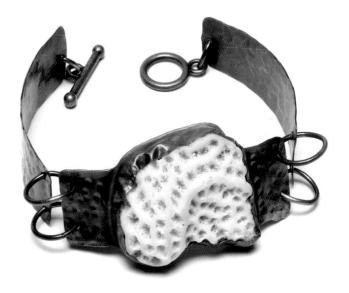

Solar System Earrings

I often teach beginners how to solder sterling silver. No matter where you take your first soldering class, you will most likely be soldering a jump ring. I designed these earrings to teach the same skills, yet resulting in something a little bit more stimulating than a basic ring. **The soldering instructions are a little more detailed here than in the following projects because this is the first project in the book to involve soldering.** After you are comfortable with this project, you can add a bead in the center of the ring, change the shape and size of the rings, or use different metals; the variations could keep you busy for months. For this project, I'm using a Wall Lenk LPT-500 butane torch.

paste soldering • forming • making holes • wire wrapping • liver of sulfer patina • making earring wires

Tool Kits
- Soldering (paste)
- Patina
- Wire wrapping

Tools
- Bench block
- Chasing hammer
- Large stepped pliers
- 1.25 mm hole punch

Materials
- 12 in. 14-gauge sterling silver wire
- 6 in. 20-gauge sterling silver wire
- 6 in. 18-gauge sterling silver wire

TIP: It is good to keep a tool, such as a soldering pick, in your dominant hand so you are not tempted to reach down and touch what you are soldering by reflex.

TIP: Train yourself to use the torch in your non-dominant hand because as your skill level progresses, you will begin doing more complicated joins and will be using tools in your dominant hand.

1. Using 14-gauge wire, make two rings on each barrel of the large stepped pliers **(a)** for a total of six rings. (If you don't own this tool, use three wooden dowels: 13, 16, and 20 mm.)

2. File the burs so the ends of the rings are flush. Close each ring **(b)**.

3. Put a 2 mm ball of medium silver solder paste on the join of a ring.

4. Place the ring in the middle of the soldering board. Light the torch and hold it in your non-dominant hand. Remember that the hottest spot is at the tip of the blue flame. Don't hold the torch so close that the blue cone is touching the metal; indirect heat is more effective. Pick up the soldering pick or tweezers in your dominant hand. Begin slowly circling the ring with the flame to bring the ring up to temperature **(c)**. Silver is a heat conductor; it will need to be heated all the way around before the solder will flow.

5. When the silver ring begins to change color, concentrate the flame on the spot to be joined **(d)**. The flux in the silver solder paste will flare up. Don't remove the flame, or the solder will form a hard shell and won't flow. Keep the flame gently moving over the join. Within 30 seconds of the flare-up dying down, the solder should flow. Remember, the solder will follow the heat, so work that to your advantage. Draw the solder in the direction you want it to flow by moving the flame.

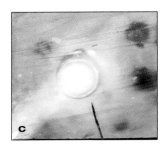
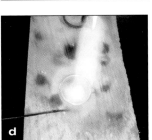
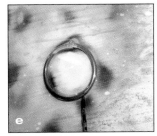

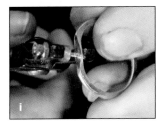
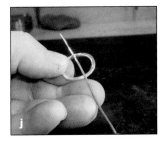
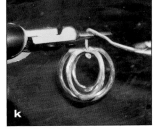

6. Remove the heat **(e)**, let the ring cool slightly, flip it over, and reheat the join to make sure the solder has completely closed the join **(f)**.

7. Cool for a few seconds, and then pickle, rinse, and brass brush.

8. Repeat Steps 3–7 with the remaining rings.

9. Place a ring on the bench block and gently hammer to texture **(g)**. Repeat with all the rings.

10. Put a ring on the ring mandrel and flatten one

section wide enough for a 1.25 mm hole **(h)**. Repeat with each ring.

11. Punch a hole in each ring in the center of each paddled section using a 1.25 mm hole punch **(i)**. (You can use a drill for this, but you will need to put the ring on a wooden dowel so the ring will not collapse during drilling.)

12. Cut two 3-in. pieces of 18-gauge sterling silver wire. Draw a bead on one end of each wire to make headpins. Pickle, rinse, and brass brush.

13. On the headpin, thread the smallest ring through the inside center **(j)**, followed by the medium, and then the large.

14. Make a basic wire-wrapped loop, wrapping the coil all the way down to the rings **(k, l)**. Repeat Steps 13–14 to make a second earring.

15. Place the earrings in a warm liver of sulfer solution to patina.

16. Make a pair of earring wires from 20-gauge wire and attach the dangles.

Sweat Soldered Negative Space Earrings

Necessity is the mother of invention, and when the price of sterling silver skyrocketed, I started to work with mixed metals. I went through my scrap box and found some sterling silver chain links that had been cut from spools of chain we sold in our bead store. It always killed me that we lost one link every time someone wanted a couple of feet of chain. So I saved them for a rainy day. Well, my rainy day came. I started sweat soldering those mismatched links of chain to copper and sawing out the centers, and this design was born— a perfect sweat-soldering project for beginners.

sweat soldering • using a jeweler's saw • texturing • making earring wires • patina

Tool Kits
- Soldering (paste)
- Texturing
- Sawing
- Patina

Tools
- Medium stepped pliers
- Large stepped pliers
- Chasing hammer
- Files and sanding sponge
- Bench block
- 1.25 mm hole punch

Materials
- **2** ¾ x 2-in. pieces of 24-gauge copper sheet
- 6 in. 14-gauge sterling silver wire
- 6 in. 20-gauge sterling silver wire

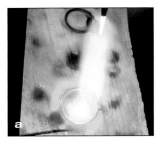

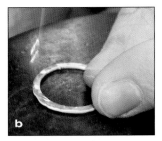

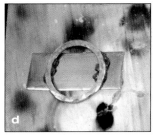

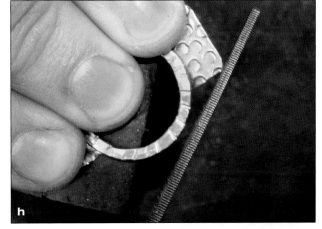

1. Use the medium barrel of large stepped pliers to make two jump rings out of the 14-gauge sterling silver wire.

2. File the ends flat and close the jump rings.

3. Refer back to page 25 to review the basics of soldering with solder paste. Solder both jump rings closed with easy solder **(a)**.

4. Place a soldered jump ring on a bench block and hammer it flat. Repeat with the other jump ring **(b)**.

5. Place six 2 mm balls of medium silver solder paste on one side of a silver ring **(c)**. Place the silver ring, solder side down, in the center of the copper sheet **(d)**. Begin heating around the outer edge of the

copper sheet with the torch (about three to four circles around).

6. Bring the heat in to the silver ring, and continue heating **(e)**. After the flux flares up and dies off, the silver solder paste should flow within 30 seconds. When you see the shimmer of the solder flowing, pull the flame off. If you keep the flame on the ring too long, the silver solder will flow out from under the ring and show on your copper sheet.

7. Cool, pickle, rinse, and brass brush.

8. Repeat Steps 5–7 with the other copper sheet and silver ring.

9. Thread a 3/0 jeweler's saw blade through the hole and load the blade in the

saw **(f)**. Saw along the inner edge of the silver ring to remove the copper. Repeat with the other earring.

10. Texture the earrings on the bench block.

11. File the edges of the two pieces of copper to slightly round the corners **(g, h)**. Use a coarse sanding sponge to remove the sharp edges of the copper sheet.

12. Patina with liver of sulfur.

13. Punch a hole in the top center of the copper **(i)**. Attach a pair of earring wires made from 20-gauge wire.

Floating Bead Bangle

I love bangles. I wear a half dozen or more on my right wrist every day. Another thing I love is JoAnne Zekowski's lampworked beads. **Put the two together and you have just about the perfect piece of jewelry as far as I'm concerned.** Jo's beads are so organic that most people don't usually even realize that they are made of glass. She has a truly original style.

soldering • texturing • using a bracelet mandrel

TIP: I use an RV sewage-line hose clamp that I purchased at Walmart. See "Kim's Unconventional Tools" to learn about using the bangle measurement tool.

Tool Kits
- Soldering (paste)
- Patina

Tools
- Anvil or bench block
- Ball-peen hammer
- Bracelet mandrel
- Bracelet bending pliers
- Bangle gauge
- Measuring tape
- File or flex shaft with Cratex wheel

Materials
- 8¼ in. 14-gauge sterling silver wire, depending on the bangle size
- Bead with 2.5 mm hole

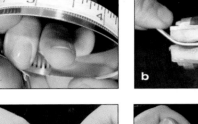

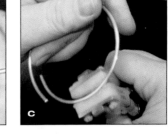
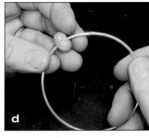
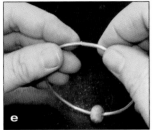
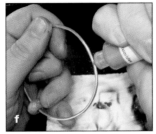

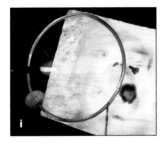

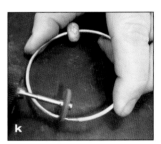

1. Determine how much wire you need by using a bangle measuring tool **(a)**. Cut the wire to the appropriate length and file the ends of the wire flat on both ends.

2. Use bracelet bending pliers or a bracelet mandrel to form a circle with the wire **(b, c)**.

3. String a bead on the wire **(d)**. Make sure that it is a bead that can resist a fair amount of heat, such as glass or hard stone.

4. Align the wire ends as closely as possible. If necessary, file the ends for a better fit **(e)**.

5. Put a 2 mm ball of solder on the join **(f)**.

6. Place the bangle on a soldering board with the bead hanging over the edge of the board. With a torch, begin moving a medium flame around the wire, gently heating up the entire bracelet **(g, h)**. Do not linger near the bead.

7. Move the flame to the area around the solder join and begin heating. After the solder flares and dies back down, it should flow within 30 seconds.

8. Turn the bangle over and briefly heat the join again to ensure the solder flows all the way through the join **(i)**.

9. Grasp the bracelet near the bead and dip the bracelet in the pickle while holding the bead out of the pickle **(j)**, then rotate the bangle around to pickle the other side. Make sure not to touch the pickle with the stainless steel tweezers. Rinse and brass brush.

10. Use a flex shaft with a Cratex brown wheel or a file to remove any excess solder **(k)**.

11. Place the bracelet on the bench block with the bead hanging over the edge and gently texture with a lightweight ball-peen hammer **(l)**.

12. Use a warm liver of sulfur solution, if desired.

Basic Sterling Silver Chain

This basic sterling silver bracelet-length chain is understated and elegant. This project is a good way to practice soldering and have a beautiful piece of jewelry at the end. The materials here make a 7½-in. bracelet. You can also make a necklace-length chain to wear by itself, or to wear with one of the pendants you have made. Use round, half-round, square, or twisted wire to make links. The wire style will alter the chain's look. **This project uses silver solder sheet simply to demonstrate how chip soldering with sheet is done.** It can be made just as easily with silver solder paste. Both solders are equally efficient: It is really just a matter of which type you prefer.

TIP: A vise makes the job of sawing the jump rings much easier because it frees up one of your hands.

pick soldering with silver solder sheet • making jump rings with a jeweler's saw

Tool Kits
- Soldering (sheet)
- Sawing

Tools
- Anvil or bench block
- Ball-peen hammer
- Bracelet mandrel
- Bracelet bending pliers
- Bangle gauge
- Measuring tape

- File or flex shaft with Cratex wheel
- Wooden dowel or carpenters pencil
- Vise
- Drill
- File or flex shaft
- Metal shears
- Two pairs of flatnose pliers
- Tumbler or cleaning cloth

Materials
- 30 in. 18-gauge sterling silver round wire, depending on the length of the chain
- Painter's tape
- Toggle bar

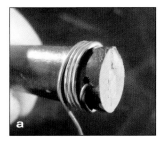

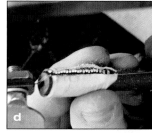

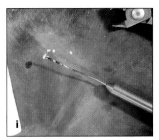

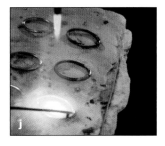

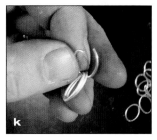

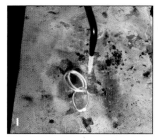

1. Choose a mandrel that's shaped as you'd like your rings. (A carpenters pencil makes oval jump rings.) Drill a hole in the top edge of the mandrel. (For 18-gauge wire, drill a 1 mm hole.)

2. Put the end of the wire in the hole and begin coiling **(a)**. The hole keeps the wire from turning while coiling. Wind the wire around the mandrel enough times to make 16 rings. Keep the wire tightly wound for uniform jump rings.

3. Tape the coil in place with painter's tape **(b)**.

4. Lock the mandrel in a vise. Hold the jump rings in place with your non-dominant hand. Saw through the tape, wire, and mandrel at an angle **(c)**. Continue to pin the coil with your non-dominant hand. You'll feel the last jump

ring separate when the entire coil **(d)** is sawn through.

5. Remove the tape and separate the jump rings **(e)**. File any burs.

6. Use flatnose pliers to close each jump ring. The jump rings must be completely closed to solder them shut. Brush flux on the joins **(f)**.

7. Cut a 1 mm pallion from a square of medium solder (see page 26) **(g)**. Cup the solder square in the palm of your hand as you cut **(h)**.

8. Place a pallion on the soldering board on the side of your dominant hand. (You don't want to reach across the flame to pick up a pallion.)

9. Holding the torch in your non-dominant hand, begin heating the jump ring. The

flux will begin to bubble and turn glassy. Move the flame to the pallion. When it balls up, touch the tip of the pick to the ball. The pallion will stick to the end of the pick **(i)**.

10. Gently reheat the jump ring and place the solder ball on the join **(j)**. Continue to heat the join until you see the solder flow. Pickle and rinse.

11. Repeat with another jump ring. When you feel comfortable, line several rings up on the board and space solder pallions along the side. Solder half the links closed.

12. Link the first and second soldered jump ring together with a third jump ring **(k)**. Solder the joining ring **(l)**. Make three sections of three.

13. Link two sections of three together with a seventh ring.

Solder the connecting ring. Add another section of three and solder the connecting ring. Add links until your chain is the desired length **(m)**.

14. Use a flex shaft or file to remove any excess solder. If there are gaps, cut the jump ring, realign it, and solder again. Solder will not fill gaps, so it would do no good to just add more solder.

15. Attach a clasp. If you have a tumbler, tumble the chain for an hour to polish and work-harden. If you don't have a tumbler, clean with a brass brush and cloth.

Old Bones Ring

A friend bought a ring similar to this one from a vendor that specializes in African antique beads, art, furniture, and tapestries. When she showed it to me I was instantly inspired by it. **I loved its simplicity and design potential.** I made one and showed it to my daughter. She immediately saw "old bones" (thus the name). I have a thing for bones!

TIP: Roll the wires between two bench blocks to straighten them. This is also a great way to work-harden wire.

(If you use fine silver, you will not need to pickle or sand the balls.)

drawing a bead on sterling silver wire • soldering

Tool Kits
- Soldering (paste)
- Patina

Tools
- Ruler
- Ring size table
- Wire cutters
- Ring mandrel
- Soft blow hammer (rubber, rawhide, nylon)
- Flex shaft with Cratex knife wheel
- Nylon-jaw pliers

Materials
- 19 in. 16-gauge sterling or fine silver wire (depending on desired ring size)

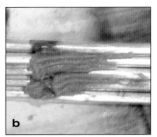

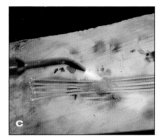

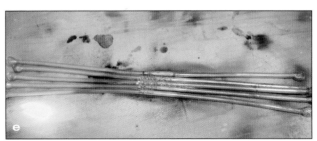

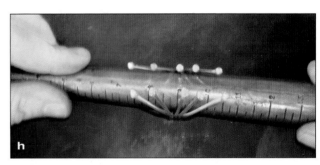

1. Use the ring size chart (page 38) to determine the length of wire needed to make your ring. Add about 1½ in. and cut five pieces of 16-gauge wire to that length. (Example: a size 7 ring requires 2¼ in. of wire. Add 2¼ in.+1½ in. = 3¾-in. length of wire x 5 pieces = total wire needed.) Keep in mind that the over-lap length is a variable that you can decide on.

2. Draw a bead on each end of each wire. Pickle and use the flex shaft to smooth out the ends of the balls.

3. Place all five pieces of wire on the soldering board with the centers touching and the ends even **(a)**. Place two 2 mm balls of medium solder paste in the center between each set of wires **(b)**.

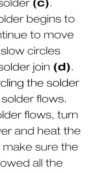

4. Use a medium flame. Remember to preheat the wires as you move in toward the solder **(c)**. When the solder begins to flare up, continue to move the flame in slow circles around the solder join **(d)**. Continue circling the solder join until the solder flows. Once the solder flows, turn the wires over and heat the join again to make sure the solder has flowed all the way through **(e)**.

5. Pickle, rinse, and brass brush the wires.

6. Use the flex shaft to remove any solder lumps on the ring.

7. Place the center of the wires on a ring mandrel at the notch of the size ring you are intending to make and bend them into a U shape **(f–h)**.

8. Wrap one balled wire end over the mandrel. Wrap the next wire from the opposite side over the mandrel **(i)**. Continue to weave the wires over the ring mandrel **(j)**.

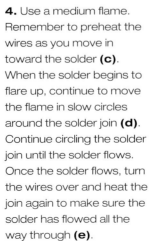

9. Pull the wires snugly against the mandrel to work-harden them into place.

10. Place the ring in a warm liver of sulfur solution; rinse, dry, and polish with 0000 steel wool.

Copper Coral Bracelet

There's nothing quite like a beach after a storm. On one such occasion in Pompano Beach, Florida, my family and I found such amazing coral washed up on shore I felt like a gambler who had hit the jackpot. I combined the coral we found that day with my favorite metal and the results speak for themselves. **The beauty of this project is that you can substitute stone, shell, bone, wood, or found objects—really anything semi-flat—for the coral.**

basic soldering • using a jeweler's saw • liver of sulfur patina

Tool Kits
- Soldering (paste)
- Sawing
- Patina

Tools
- Flex shaft with Cratex knife wheel
- Bracelet mandrel
- Bracelet bending pliers
- Soft blow hammer (rubber, rawhide, nylon)
- Files and sanding sponge
- Medium stepped pliers
- Hole punch or drill
- Half a clothespin or burnisher
- Wire cutters
- Dental floss

Materials
- Coral or other found object focal approximately 21–51 mm wide, with edges 2–3 mm shorter than the bezel wire
- 3 x 5-in. piece of 24-gauge copper sheet (depending on the focal)
- ¼-in. copper bezel wire to fit around focal
- 6 in. 16-gauge copper wire
- 6 in. any gauge steel binding wire (depending on the size focal)
- Toggle clasp

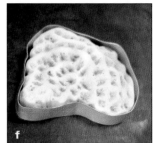

1. Form the bezel wire around the stone. Cut the bezel wire with metal shears so the ends meet perfectly **(a)**.

2. Align the bezel wire so that the two ends meet for soldering **(b)**.

3. Place a 2 mm ball of easy solder paste between the two ends and place them back together **(c)**.

4. Place the bezel in the center of the soldering board. Using a medium flame, begin circling the bezel on the outside edge. When the solder flares up, continue moving the flame in, gradually bringing the flame inside the bezel wire. Concentrate on the join.

5. When the solder flows, remove the flame, flip the bezel over, and reheat the join, drawing the solder throughout the entire join **(d)**.

6. Pickle, rinse, and brass brush.

7. Use a flex shaft to smooth out the solder join both inside and out **(e)**.

8. Reshape the bezel around the stone and gently remove, making sure not to distort the shape **(f)**.

9. Place the bezel on the copper sheet and cut out a base that is ¾ in. larger in diameter than the bezel wire. The bezel must lie flat against the sheet all the way around. If the bezel is not flat against the sheet, it will not solder to the sheet **(g)**. If the sheet is not flat or the bezel is not flat, use a soft blow hammer and gently flatten each piece.

TIP Place the bezel on a mirror to see if all the edges rest on the mirror.

10. Place 2 mm balls of easy solder paste all the way around the inside bottom edge of the bezel wire, spaced ⅛ in. apart **(h)**. Replace the bezel on the sheet.

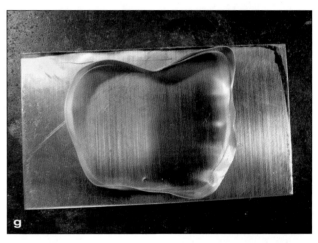

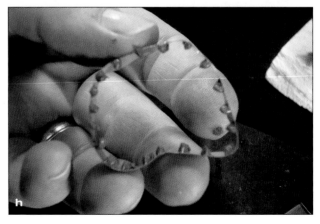

11. Begin soldering by moving a medium flame around the outer edge of the bezel wire, gently heating up the copper sheet. Remember: heat

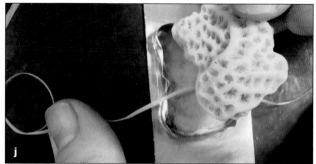

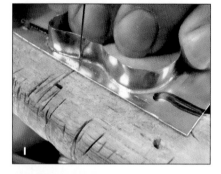

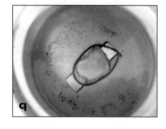

big first. The sheet will draw most of the heat, so it must be heated up first **(i)**.

12. Continue to heat the piece until the solder flows. If the bezel appears to rise, hold it down with a soldering pick. Be careful to not lift one side while holding down the opposite. This can start a vicious cycle. You may cause the bezel to shift and spread solder to unwanted spots on the sheet, or cause the bezel to lose its shape.

13. Check all the way around the bezel to ensure that all of the edges are soldered down. You should see a thin line of solder flowing out from underneath the bezel evenly all the way around.

14. Pickle, rinse, and brass brush.

15. Check the base of the bezel for any lifting. If it has not soldered down completely, apply extra-easy solder paste and reheat.

16. Pickle, rinse, and brass brush.

17. Place a piece of dental floss across the bezel. Set

the stone in to check the fit. Pull both ends of the dental floss to remove the stone **(j)**. If the stone doesn't fit, reheat and lift the bezel off the sheet to reshape it. Then resolder the bezel.

18. Once you're satisfied with your bezel, use a permanent marker to draw tabs for the bracelet **(k)**.

19. Using a jeweler's saw with a 3/0 blade, cut around the bezel and the bracelet tabs **(l)**.

20. Use a flex shaft to remove unwanted solder and metal **(m)**. (If there's a lot of metal around the edges after sawing, filing may be quicker and more effective than using the flex shaft.)

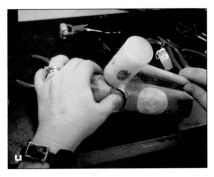

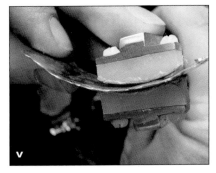

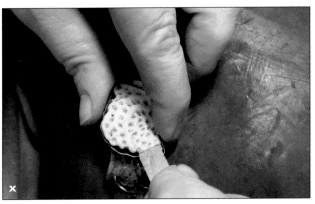

21. Using metal shears, cut two pieces of copper the same width as the tabs on the bezel to complete the bracelet **(n)**.

22. Use a file and a sanding sponge to smooth all the edges **(o)**.

23. Make a steel binding wire ring around the bezel and put the bezel and the steel binding wire in the pickle solution. (See page 36.) Leave it in for a few minutes for a good plating of copper on any solder that may be showing on the exterior of the bezel **(p, q)**.

24. Rinse and brass brush.

25. Texture the tabs and the bracelet sections **(r)**.

26. Use a spring-loaded punch to dimple the spots where you are going to drill holes to attach jump rings to connect all the components of the bracelet (two on each tab and one each for the toggle) **(s)**.

27. Make a ⅟₁₆-in. hole in each dimple **(t)**. File any burs.

28. Use a soft blow hammer and a bracelet mandrel to shape the

bracelet flaps **(u)**. Use bracelet bending pliers to shape the side pieces **(v)**.

29. Using the largest barrel of stepped pliers (or a dowel) make four 10 mm jump rings out of 16-gauge copper wire.

30. Attach the bracelet pieces to the bezel pieces **(w)**.

31. Place the bracelet in a warm liver of sulfur solution. Rinse, dry, and polish with 0000 steel wool.

32. Set the stone in the bezel. Make sure that it is

lying as snugly in the bezel as possible. Use half a clothespin to push the sides of the bezel down. Picturing an imaginary compass, start at the southernmost point of the bezel, move to the northern most point, then eastern, then western. Continue this process until you have completely pushed the bezel down over the stone **(x)**.

33. Use a burnisher to tighten the bezel down over the stone **(y)**.

34. Finish by attaching a clasp.

Turtle Bezel Line Fold

Because I teach at The William Holland School of Lapidary Arts, many of my students have a lapidary background instead of a beading or jewelry design background. They come to me wanting to use stones that they have found on a mineral club field trip. They don't want to use the traditional soldered bezel method or wire wrapping technique. They're looking for something unique and different. **This project teaches a low-tech, attractive way to attach virtually anything to a metal backplate to create a pendant.** I call it a turtle bezel. Line form foldforming is an easy way to texture the metal backplate. The textured surface holds patina so the texture really stands out. You can combine two great things—the turtle bezel and line form foldforming—and get a great pendant.

foldforming • using a jeweler's saw • cold connections • liver of sulfur patina

Tool Kits
- Foldforming
- Sawing
- Cold connections
- Patina

Tools
- Soft blow hammer
- Marker
- Half a clothespin or burnisher
- Hole punch or drill
- Flatnose pliers
- Roundnose pliers

Materials
- Approximately 8 x 12 mm cabochon
- 3 x 5-in. piece of 24-gauge copper sheet, depending on the cabochon
- 2 $\frac{1}{16}$-in. tube rivets
- 2 $\frac{1}{8}$-in. commercial eyelets

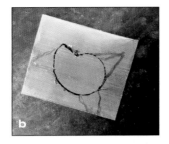
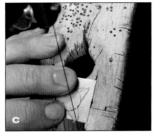
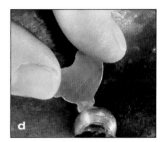

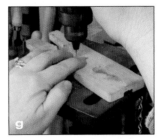
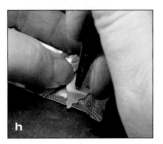
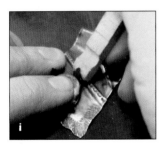

1. Trace the shape or outline of your stone on the copper. Leave enough margin to draw in tabs **(a)**.

2. Draw at least three tabs outside the stone's outline. You can add more tabs as part of your design. I usually cut tabs about the height of the edge of the stone plus ⅛ in. The tabs can be shortened when the stone is set if they are too long. Drawing the tabs is not a precise science. I usually just eyeball how long to draw the tabs or make a paper template and measure it against the stone **(b)**.

3. Use a jeweler's saw with a 3/0 blade to cut out the "turtle tabs" **(c)**.

4. Texture the backs of the tabs **(d)**. (The tabs are going to be folded up and over the stone, exposing the backs.)

5. Texture a piece of copper using the line fold technique (page 27). Cut it about three times larger than your turtle tab **(e)**. File the corners and sand the edges of the line fold with a coarse sanding sponge.

6. Place the turtle tab on the pendant and use a punch to dimple two spots for tube rivets through the turtle tab and the pendant **(f)**.

7. Drill two ¹⁄₁₆-in. holes in the turtle tab and one ¹⁄₁₆-in. hole in the pendant **(g)**.

8. Attach the turtle bezel to the pendant using ¹⁄₁₆-in. tube rivets. Drill the second hole using the original hole in the tab as a guide for the second hole in the base piece. Set the second tube rivet **(h)**.

9. Use flatnose pliers (or a clothespin tool) to gently bend the tabs up to a 90° angle.

10. Place the pendant in a warm liver of sulfur solution; rinse and dry.

11. Place the stone on the turtle bezel and fold the tabs up against the side of the stone **(i)**.

12. Use half of a clothespin to burnish the tabs over the stone **(j)**.

13. Use roundnose pliers to roll the top of the pendant into a tube bail **(k)**.

14. Use a soft blow hammer and the end of a

punch positioned against the rolled tube to flatten the pendant **(l)**.

15. Remove excess patina with 0000 steel wool to highlight the texture **(m)**. Choose more or less patina, depending on the color of your stone.

Explosion Prong Pendant

The beauty of this pendant is that you can set anything, or any shape, in it. I've set images under resin, glass and stone cabochons, taxidermy eyeballs, and charms. **The explosion prong method is quite versatile and adapts easily to unconventional shapes.** In other versions, I've lashed the two pieces together rather than rivet them. The sky is the limit.

TIP: This is a good project for rolling mill texture if you have a mill. You can texture the sheet prior to cutting out the disks or after.

cold connections • cutting negative space with a jeweler's saw • drawing a bead on wire • liver of sulfur patina

Tool Kits
- Cold connections
- Sawing
- Patina

Tools
- Disk cutter
- Torch
- Tweezers
- Half a clothespin or burnisher
- Flex shaft, drill press, or other machine drill
- Metal shears
- Files
- Spring-loaded punch

Materials
- 4 x 2-in. piece of 24-gauge copper sheet
- 10 in. 16-gauge sterling silver wire
- Stone or found object for setting

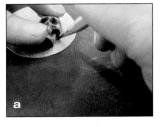

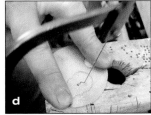

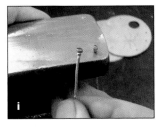

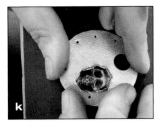

11. When you are happy with the placement of your object in the prongs, attach a nail-head rivet through both disks. Hang the prong setting over the edge of the anvil and set the rivet **(l)**.

1. Cut two 2-in. disks from copper sheet. Texture as desired. File and smooth any rough edges.

2. At the top of each disk punch a ½-in. diameter hole. (If you don't have a disk cutter, use a jeweler's saw. Review "Cutting out negative space," pages 20–21.)

3. Place the object on a disk and trace around it **(a, b)**.

4. Punch or drill a hole inside the outline. Insert a 3/0 saw blade in the hole and load the blade in the saw frame **(c)**. Saw a jagged line from one side of the outline to the other **(d)**. Back up the saw

blade to the center of the outline and saw a jagged line across to the opposite side. Continue backing your saw blade to the center and sawing across until you have jagged lines radiating from the center to points all around the outline **(e)**. (These will become the explosion prongs.) Remove the saw blade.

5. Place this disk on top of the remaining disk on a bench block **(f)**. Use a spring-loaded punch to make dimples for 5–9 holes around the outer edge **(g)**.

6. Drill all the holes in the top disk **(h)** and only one hole in the bottom disk.

7. Cut nine 2-in. pieces of 16-gauge wire and draw a bead on one end of each.

8. Place a beaded wire in an anvil or draw plate and flatten the ball to make a nail-head rivet **(i)**. (Review "Nail-head rivets," page 18.) Repeat with all the wires.

9. Use chainnose pliers to pry open the explosion prongs **(j)**.

10. Place the disks together and file away any overlapping edges. Shape the prongs around the stone, and place the top disk on the bottom disk. Press down using the bottom disk as a tension point for the object being set **(k)**.

12. Drill a hole in the bottom disk **(m)** using the top disk as a guide and set another rivet. Continue drilling holes and setting the rest of the rivets **(n)**.

13. Use a clothespin or burnisher to fold the prongs over the stone **(o)**. File the disks so the shapes match. Sometimes they shift ever-so-slightly during drilling and riveting. This is not an exercise in perfection, but anything that draws attention away from the explosion should be filed.

14. Place the pendant in a warm liver of sulfur solution, rinse, dry, and polish with 0000 steel wool.

Urban Pinecone Pendant

Have you ever tried to make jewelry from pinecones? They are adorable, but quite fragile. I've tried wiring them to a pendant, and I've even tried to coat one in resin, but nothing worked. A disk cutter, a dapping block, and some copper later, though, and I've got a tiny pinecone that will last forever.

texturing • disk cutter • dapping block • basic wire wrapping • rolling mill

Tool Kits
- Patina
- Texturing
- Wirewrapping

Tools
- Disk cutter or circle template
- Center finder (page 36)
- Domed chasing hammer
- Bench block
- Metal shears
- Hole punch or drill
- Dapping block
- Medium stepped pliers or wooden dowel

Materials
- 1 x 5-in. piece of 24-gauge copper sheet
- 12 in. 18-gauge steel binding wire
- **50** 1-mm thick flat spacer disks with holes large enough for 18-gauge wire
- Renaissance wax

OPTIONS:
Create a binding wire chain to hang the pinecone on.

Make a smaller set as earrings.

Use a rolling mill or texture hammers and stamps on the disks.

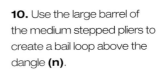

1. Use a disk cutter or a template to cut five disks, graduated in size: 1, ⅞, ¾, ⅝, and ½ in. **(a)**.

2. Gently texture each disk, trying not to distort the shape of the circle (a little distortion makes them look more organic). This is a good project for the rolling mill **(b)**.

3. Smooth the edges of the disks with a coarse sanding sponge, rubbing over the edges of both the front and the back of each disk **(c)**.

4. Locate the center of each disk **(d)**, mark, and dimple for a future hole. Dap each disk with a dapping block. Start in a hole larger than the disk and work your way down to one close in size **(e)**.

5. Drill a ¹⁄₁₆-in. hole in the center of each disk **(f)**. Gently file away the burs **(g)**.

6. Place the disks in a warm liver of sulfer solution to patina.

7. Cut a 6-in. piece of 18-gauge binding wire. Clean and prepare the binding wire (see page 16).

8. Place one end of the binding wire on the bench block and, using a chasing hammer, make a paddle on the end **(h)**.

9. String: five flat spacers, the smallest domed disk, five flat spacers, and the next largest disk. Continue alternating five spacers and a disk, ending with the 1-in. disk **(i–m)**.

10. Use the large barrel of the medium stepped pliers to create a bail loop above the dangle **(n)**.

11. Wrap the wire tail down to the top of the dome **(o)**.

12. Place the loop you just made on the anvil with the coils hanging over the edge. Hammer the loop flat with a domed chasing hammer **(p)**. String the pendant as desired.

Basket Weave Ring

One year, our booth at the huge annual Tucson gem show was across from a young man selling African beads, artwork, and tapestries. I really liked a ring he had because it was not gender specific. I've modified the design for this project, but the original influence is evident. **I've made this ring several ways, changing it each time to use materials that I already had available.** In the first version, I soldered two pieces of 8-gauge low-dome wire together, then sawed it apart to create the paddles. The second time I made this ring, I soldered two pieces of 11-gauge square wire together then sawed it apart. I was equally pleased with both, but using double half-round wire is much easier.

using a jeweler's saw • forging

Tool Kits
- Sawing
- Patina

Tools
- Ring sizing chart
- Ruler
- Domed chasing hammer
- Anvil or bench block
- Soft blow hammer
- Files
- Flex shaft with brown Cratex wheel
- Knife

Materials
- 4-in. wide double half-round wire (depending on the size of your ring)

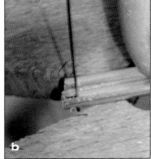

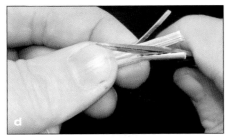

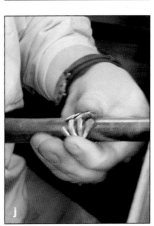

1. Use the ring size chart (page 38) to determine the length of wire needed to make your ring, and add 1 in. to that measurement. (Example: a size 7 ring = 2¼ in. + 1 in. or 3¼ in.) Use a jeweler's saw to cut the wire to length **(a)**.

2. Center and mark the length of the ring shaft on the wires. Subtract ¼ in from each mark and remark the ring (Example: size 7 = 2¼ in. Subtract ¼ in. from each side and you now have a 1¾-in. ring shank marked).

3. On each end, saw the double wire in half with a jeweler's saw, stopping at the lines made in step 2 **(b, c)**. Saw each half in half again. Separate the wires with a knife **(d, e)**.

4. Using a chasing hammer and an anvil or bench block, flatten all four ends and gently texture the ring shaft **(f)**. Repeat on the other end.

5. File any burs **(g)**.

6. Place the middle of the wires on a ring mandrel at the size needed and bend the ends up into a U **(h, i)**.

7. Pull an end wire up and over the ring mandrel. Pull the wire on the opposite side of the ring up and over the ring mandrel **(j)**. Continue weaving the wires.

8. Use a soft blow hammer to work-harden the wires in place **(k)**.

9. Place the ring in a warm liver of sulfur solution, rinse, dry, and polish with 0000 steel wool.

Nightmare Catcher

I love bones, ghosts, cemeteries, vampires, and witches even though they scare the bejesus out of me. When I was a child, I was such a chicken that I usually slept with my brother who is seven years younger than me. Our dad convinced us that if we slept with the sheets up over our shoulders vampires couldn't get us. Neither of us to this day can sleep with our shoulders bare. **When my daughter was young she had a really bad dream one night, and I made her a "nightmare" catcher.** She kept it hanging over her bed for years. She named this piece for me. I hope it works for you.

wire weaving • using a jeweler's saw • liver of sulfur patina

Tool Kits
- Sawing
- Patina
- Cold connections
- Wirewrapping

Tools
- Spring-loaded punch
- Hole punch or drill press
- Files
- Skull template
- Bicycle spoke or mandrel
- Coarse sanding sponge and 0000 steel wool

Materials
- 24-gauge copper sheet
- 26-gauge steel binding wire
- 14-gauge copper wire
- Adhesive paper
- Pencil and paper
- **2** large jump rings
- Crystal

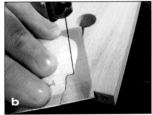

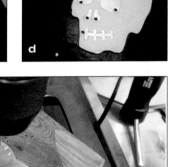

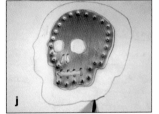

1. Make a skull pattern on adhesive paper using a punch, a freehand drawing, or clip art. Adhere to the 24-gauge copper sheet **(a)**.

2. Use a jeweler's saw and 3/0 saw blade to cut out the skull **(b)**.

3. Use a spring-loaded punch to dimple each part of the skull face to be sawn out **(c)**. Drill or punch a hole in each dimple **(d)**.

4. Thread the saw blade through a hole and saw out the negative space. Continue sawing to complete the face **(e)**.

5. Use a spring-loaded punch to make dimples around the edge of the skull, about ⅛ in. apart. Position

the dimples close to the edge, but not so close that the hole might run off **(f)**.

6. Drill or punch each hole **(g)**. File all of the drill hole burs from the back **(h)**.

7. Place the skull on a mat and sand with a coarse sanding sponge **(i)**.

8. Place the skull on a piece of paper and trace an outline that is ¼ in. larger **(j)**.

9. Using the drawn outline as a guide, bend the 14-gauge wire **(k)**.

10. Prepare one yard of 26-gauge binding wire (page 16). Coil the wire tightly on a bicycle spoke or other 14-gauge mandrel **(l)**.

11. Slide the coil off of the mandrel and thread it onto the 14-gauge copper wire skull outline, making sure that the opening of the outline is threaded into the coil, binding the two ends together **(m, n)**. Repeat Step 10 to cover the copper wire (I used about 3 yards in this project). Cut and prepare one yard of binding wire. Coil the end around

the outline coil and secure the wire into the coils of the original **(o)**.

12. Thread one end of the 26-gauge wire into one of the holes drilled into the edge of the skull **(p)**. Make one loop over the coiled wire frame. Thread the wire through the next hole in the

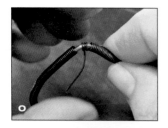

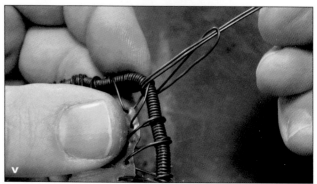

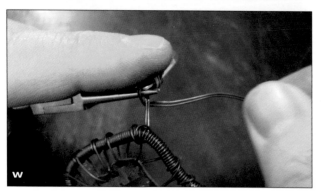

skull from the back and go back up and loop it around the coiled frame. Continue threading and looping all the way around the skull outline **(q–s)**. Make sure not to pull the wire too tight or you will not get an even catcher. Your goal is to keep a ¼-in. space between the skull and the coiled frame. When you have woven the wire all the way around the skull outline, wrap the end around the coiled frame in three tight loops, integrating the loops into the original coil **(t)**.

13. Make two large 18-gauge binding wire or other wire jump rings to attach to the top of the catcher to connect the chain **(u)**.

14. Place the catcher in a warm liver of sulfur solution, rinse, dry, and polish with 0000 steel wool.

15. Use 26-gauge binding wire to attach a clear natural crystal onto the bottom of your nightmare catcher to store all your captured nightmares **(v, w)**.

Three-Dimensional Tree Pendant

One of my students brought this awesome paper punch that was a tree without leaves. I immediately saw the possibility of a great sawing activity for one of my advanced students named Lorna. **It just so happened that she had a stone her husband cut for her that was faceted in such a way that it could not be set in a conventional prong basket.** We were trying to think of a cold connection that could be used to set the stone. When I saw all the great limbs of this tree, I immediately thought, "prongs." Here's a version for you to try.

sawing • piercing • green and blue patina • cold connections

Tool Kits
- Cold connections
- Sawing
- Patina

Tools
- Metal shears
- Roundnose pliers

Materials
- **2** 3 x 3-in. pieces of 24-gauge copper sheet
- Leafless tree template
- Small cabochon
- **4** .080 micro screws and nuts to fit
- **12** 8 mm spacers with ¹⁄₁₆-in. holes
- **2** #2 iron-cut tacks
- **2** ⅛-in. eyelets

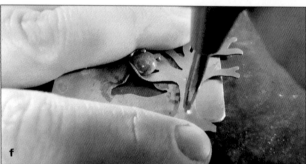

1. Cut two 2½ x 2½-in. pieces of 24-gauge sheet metal.

2. Choose a design to use for your project. This design can be hand drawn, stamp transferred, or from a sticker outline.

3. Apply the image to a metal square. This will become the top component **(a, b)**.

4. Use a spring-loaded punch to make a dimple in the metal in an inconspicuous place on the image and drill, or punch a 1.25 mm hole.

5. Thread the saw blade through the hole and load the jeweler's saw.

6. Begin sawing the outside edge of the image. Remember to hold the saw gently and to saw in graceful up-and-down strokes with your middle finger in front of the blade and your index finger behind the blade. Turn the metal (not the saw blade) to saw curves, as you continue to gently move the blade up and down.

7. When the image is pierced out of the metal, separate both pieces and use a coarse sanding sponge to remove sharp edges **(c)**. If there are any burs, gently remove them with a jeweler's file.

8. Shape the branches so they will hold the cabochon **(d)**. Remove the stone.

9. Texture the second metal square (back plate) as desired **(e)**.

10. Place the back plate, the pierced piece, and the tree in a warm liver of sulfur (or other patina) solution. Retrieve the pieces, dry, and remove unwanted color with 0000 steel wool. (Sand each piece to a different level of patina.)

11. Seal with Renaissance wax or acrylic spray.

12. Place the cut-out tree over the open tree. (Lay it flat, or add washers between the two layers to add height to the top piece and create a shadow effect.)

13. Dimple the spots you need to drill, and drill or punch the holes in the top component, but only one hole in the bottom component **(f, g)**.

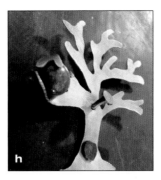

14. Choose the rivet material that best suits your design **(h)**. Place a spacer on each rivet to create height **(i)**. Trim, file, and rivet the cut-out tree in place **(j)**.

15. Use roundnose pliers to shape the branches of the

tree for a three-dimensional effect **(k)**.

16. Align the component with the tree attached to the bottom plate **(l)**.

17. Dimple and drill a hole at each corner **(m, n)**.

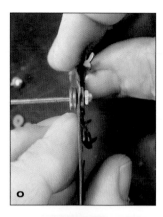

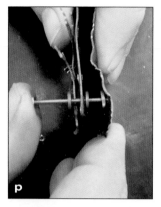

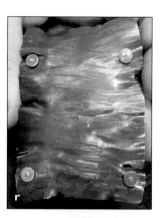

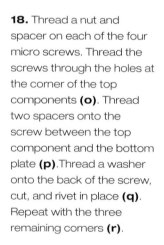

18. Thread a nut and spacer on each of the four micro screws. Thread the screws through the holes at the corner of the top components **(o)**. Thread two spacers onto the screw between the top component and the bottom plate **(p)**. Thread a washer onto the back of the screw, cut, and rivet in place **(q)**. Repeat with the three remaining corners **(r)**.

19. Dimple each of the two top corners of the base plate **(s)**.

20. Using a ⅛-in. hand punch, make a hole in each dimple **(t)**.

21. Place an eyelet (tube rivet) in each hole and set **(u, v)**.

22. Use roundnose pliers to shape the branches of the top component and reset the stone in the appropriate branches.

Chapter 3

FIRE! FIRE! FIRE! What an amazing tool! Yes I said tool. It's what separates us from the animals. Many animals use tools, but none uses fire. And look at the amazing things that we can do with the manipulation of fire. With fire, metal, and some very simple tools, we can create awesome things. But you must first overcome your fear of fire, and the first step to overcoming that fear is to learn how to manipulate the fire both safely and correctly.

In this chapter you are going to be using what I call "big fire," which is the flame from a propane or acetylene torch. You will learn how to read the fire and soon you'll know by instinct when to add more heat or back the flame off a bit. You will learn how to draw out the best possible patterns, create the most satisfying shapes, and achieve awesome color using nothing but fire. The best advice I have for this chapter is relax. Don't tense up. Make smooth, easy movements. If you can pat your head and rub your tummy, you've got it made. No sweat. (Well maybe some sweat, but not much.)

Reticulated Brass and Copper Cuff

reticulation • forming • liver of sulfur patina • annealing • cold connections

Funny how you start down the creative path in one direction and invariably take a detour for a much better destination! My original plan for this bracelet was to fold the edges of the copper up over the brass to hold it in place on the cuff, but I was so inspired by the organic movement the brass took on when I reticulated it, I felt it all needed to show. For contrast, out came my sterling silver rivets. A great piece of textured copper became the base and it all fit together perfectly! **Reticulate several pieces of brass at one time while you have the torch set up, then clean them up and stare at them for a while.** It's sort of like finding pictures in the clouds. Vary the backgrounds, add embellishments, or play with some of the patinas described on pages 32 and 33. You'll be amazed at what you'll come up with.

RETICULATING TIPS:

Place the brass sheet in the center of an annealing pan. Using a large tip on your torch (#3 tip on a Goss torch), begin heating the sheet. Continue until you see the sheet begin to melt in various spots. Use the heat and the melting process to create a pleasing texture. Hold the flame in spots to create holes, peaks, or valleys. For this project, stay away from the edges. When you are happy with the look, remove the heat. Pickle, rinse, and brass brush.

Tool Kits
- Annealing
- Patina
- Cold connections
- Texturing

Tools
- Shears
- Soft blow hammer
- Files and coarse sanding sponges
- Bracelet mandrel
- Bracelet-bending pliers (optional)

Materials
- 1½ x 6-in. piece of 24-gauge copper sheet (textured if you desire)
- 1 x 6-in. piece of 24-gauge brass sheet
- 10 in. 16-gauge sterling silver wire (depending on the number of rivets in your design)

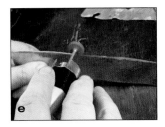

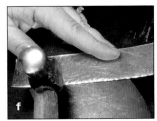

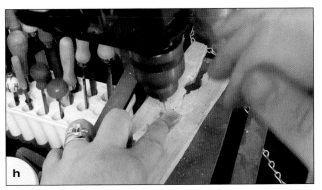

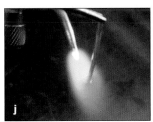

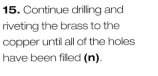

1. Cut a 1 x 6-in. piece of brass sheet **(a)**.

2. Reticulate the center, being careful to stay away from the edges **(b, c)**.

3. Don't pickle, but sand some of the firescale off.

4. Cut a 1½ x 6-in. strip of copper sheet **(d)**.

5. File the corners and round the edges of each piece of metal **(e)**.

6. Texture the copper edges **(f)** with the balled end of the ball-peen hammer.

7. Center the brass strip on the textured copper **(g)**.

8. Using a spring-loaded punch, dimple the spots

where you would like to make the attachments.

9. Drill all of the holes in the reticulated brass piece **(h)**.

10. Drill only one hole in the copper strip **(i)**.

11. Cut a 1-in. piece of 16-gauge wire for each drilled hole. Ball an end of each wire **(j)**.

12. Make nail-head rivets with each piece of balled wire **(k)**.

13. Using a nail-head rivet, attach the reticulated brass strip to the copper strip **(l)**.

14. Drill another hole in the copper base using a hole in the brass strip as a guide, and make another attachment **(m)**.

15. Continue drilling and riveting the brass to the copper until all of the holes have been filled **(n)**.

16. Shape the metal strip into a cuff by using bracelet-bending pliers or a bracelet mandrel **(o)**.

17. Add patina with a warm liver of sulfur solution. Polish **(p)**.

Reticulated Brass Pendant

I consider this pendant a diamond in the rough. The reticulated brass is unpredictable and organic, and the stone is so smooth. The two are opposite, yet they look good together. Opposites truly do attract. I've also set faceted stones on these pendants—what a statement. **Using a cabochon in a prong basket is unconventional, but it works here.** Sapphire is a hard stone and the one I used had no fracture lines, so the pressure of the prongs was not likely to break the stone.

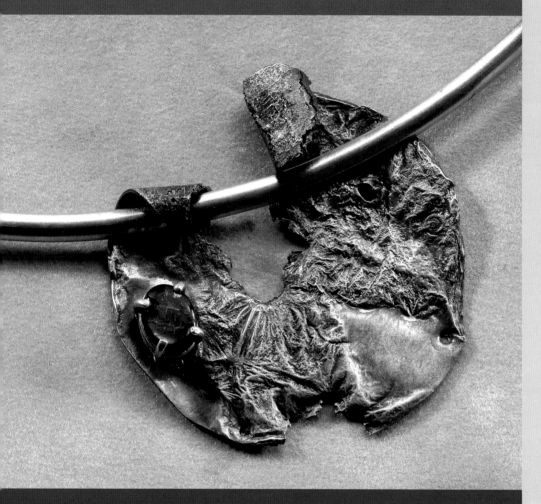

reticulation • soldering • liver of sulfur patina

TIP The brass may pick up slight copper plating if you are using an older saturated pickle solution. I prefer this look. If you do not want this, make sure you have a clean pickling solution. I consider this mixed-color look a very happy artistic moment.

Tool Kits
- Soldering
- Patina

Tools
- 1.25 mm hole punch (optional)
- Metal shears
- Prong pusher or flatnose pliers
- Files and sanding sponge

Materials
- 24-gauge brass sheet
- Pre-made sterling silver prong basket
- Stone to fit prong basket

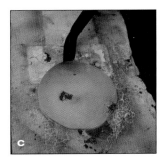

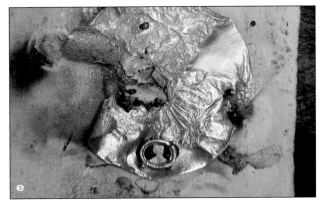

1. Cut a shape for the pendant out of the brass sheet.

2. Place the brass shape in the center of a soldering block. Using a #3 tip on the torch (a large flame), begin heating the brass. Continue heating until the brass begins to melt in various spots **(a)**.

3. Use the heat and the melting process to create a pleasing texture. Hold the flame in spots to create holes, peaks, and valleys. Melt the edges of the brass sheet to create an organic-looking shape **(b, c)**. When you are happy with the look, remove the heat. Pickle, rinse, and brass brush.

4. Use a file and/or a coarse sanding sponge to remove any sharp edges that may have appeared during reticulation.

5. Place two 2 mm balls of easy solder paste on the underside of the prong basket **(d)**. Position the basket on the pendant **(e)**.

6. With a #1 tip or a medium flame, begin heating the brass sheet. Remember heat big first: The sheet will need much more heat than the prong basket. Do not apply much heat to the prong basket or it will melt **(f)**.

7. Pickle, rinse, and brass brush **(g)**.

8. Place the stone in the prong basket. Use a prong pusher to set the prongs over the stone. Be careful to not apply too much pressure at one time or you may slip and chip the stone **(h, i)**.

9. Place the pendant in a warm liver of sulfur solution. Rinse, dry, and polish with 0000 steel wool.

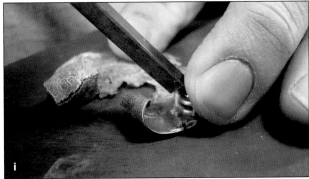

Reticulated Sterling Silver Pendant

My friend Karen spent Thanksgiving with my son and me at our beach cabin. She had just finished taking a class in surface textures, and we were eager to experiment with some of her newly acquired techniques. **We started melting all the silver we could get our hands on.** All too soon Karen had to go back to her home and job in Atlanta, but before leaving, we challenged each other to make something cool with the new pieces of textured metals we had made. I came up with a pendant similar to this project to share with her on our next visit.

reticulation • nail-head rivet • cold connections • drawing a bead

Tool Kits
- Soldering
- Annealing
- Wirewrapping
- Cold connections
- Patina

Tools
- Metal shears
- 1.8 mm hole punch or drill with 1/16-in. bit
- Round file or bead reamer
- Beading awl

Materials
- 24-gauge sterling silver disk
- 24-gauge copper disk
- 16-gauge copper wire
- Small brass washers
- Fast-drying clear glue
- Renaissance wax or acrylic spray lacquer

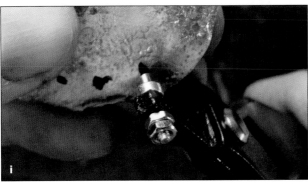

1. Review the annealing instructions (page 28). Use a medium flame to anneal the silver disk by bringing it to a low orange glow **(a)**.

TIP Mark the silver with a permanent marker and heat it until the mark disappears.

2. Pickle, rinse, and brass brush.

3. Anneal— including pickling, rinsing, and brass brushing—five times. This brings the fine silver to the surface of the sheet to create reticulation silver.

4. Now it's time to reticulate. Heat the disk until it begins to glow orange **(b, c)**. Apply heat in a circular pattern until you see the surface of the silver begin to ripple **(d)**. Contin-

ue to apply heat; raise and lower the flame to manipulate the ridges and valleys created by the flame. When you are pleased with the look of your reticulated silver disk, let it cool. Pickle, rinse, and brass brush **(e)**.

5. Cut a copper disk slightly larger than the silver disk. Texture the edges of the copper disk **(f)**.

6. Place the sterling disk on top of the copper disk slightly off center. Mark and punch two holes in the copper disk for the chain to be attached later **(g)**.

7. Punch holes in the silver disk in the spots where you want to attach rivets. This is a functional as well as decorative element, so be creative with your

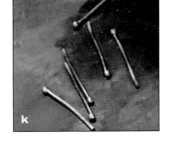

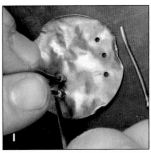

placement and number of rivets **(h, i)**.

8. Re-align the silver disk on top of the copper disk and using a scribe, mark the spots through the holes where the rivets will be placed **(j)**.

9. Use a spring-loaded punch to dimple the drill spots on the copper disk. Drill all the holes in the copper disk.

10. Place both metal pieces in a warm liver of sulfur solution. Remove excess patina with 0000 steel wool.

11. Cut six 2-in. pieces of 16-gauge copper wire. Draw a bead on an end of each piece of wire. Quench quickly in cold water to make a red ball **(k)**.

12. Thread three balled wires through three of the holes in the silver disk and thread three spacers on each wire **(l)**.

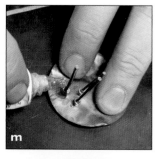

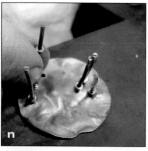

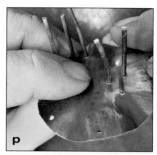

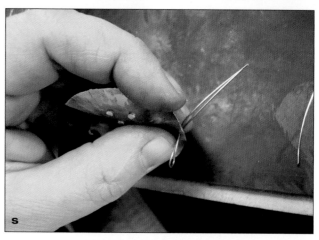

13. Put a drop of clear, fast-drying glue on each set of spacers to hold in place **(m)**. Thread the remaining wires in the remaining holes and add the washers on the back, securing them in place with a drop of glue **(n)**.

14. Place the copper disk over the copper wire rivets, making sure that each wire rivet fits the corresponding hole **(o, p)**.

15. Trim each wire 1 mm above the copper disk and file flat. Rivet each wire in place **(q, r)**. (A divot in my anvil keeps the ball from flattening.)

16. Fold a 6 in. piece of 26-gauge sterling wire in half and thread it through one of the holes in the top of the copper **(s)**.

17. Make a lark's head knot with the wires **(t)**.

18. Make a basic wire wrap with the remaining wire to make a loop bail **(u)**.

19. Repeat to complete a bail on the other hole **(v)**.

20. Protect the patina with an application of Renaissance wax or acrylic spray lacquer.

Pine Straw Casting Bezel Pendant

I had a drawing in my sketch book of a pendant that I wanted to make. I conferred with my studio buddy Dan to hear his thoughts about my idea. I made several pine straw castings. I laid them all out, chose the one I liked, got out my stone, and completely redesigned the entire pendant, not even referring to the original sketch. Oh well.

TIP You can use a MAPP gas canister torch or other torch that burns hot and bushy. I used an Goss air-acetylene torch with a #3 tip in this project.

pine straw casting • basic soldering • making a bail • bezel setting a stone

Tool Kit
- Soldering

Tools
- Casting crucible
- Graphite stick
- Metal can
- Files
- Rubber band
- Flex shaft with brown Cratex wheel

- Dental floss
- Annealing pan or fire bricks on a heat-resistant surface
- Half a clothespin or burnisher
- Ruler
- Marker
- Tumbler

Materials
- ⅓ troy oz. of clean silver scrap
- Borax or casting flux

- Long pine needles or broom straw (soak broom straw overnight)
- Water
- Small piece of 26- or 24-gauge sterling silver sheet
- 26-gauge 4 mm wide fine silver bezel wire, depending on the object to be set
- Stone or found object for pendant

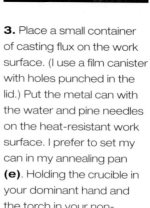
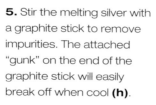
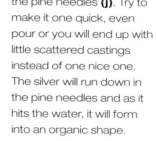

4. As the scrap begins to melt and run to the center of the crucible, put a shake of casting flux in **(g)**.

5. Stir the melting silver with a graphite stick to remove impurities. The attached "gunk" on the end of the graphite stick will easily break off when cool **(h)**.

6. When the silver forms a molten ball that moves freely around the crucible **(i)**, keep the torch on the molten ball and pour the silver into the center of the pine needles **(j)**. Try to make it one quick, even pour or you will end up with little scattered castings instead of one nice one. The silver will run down in the pine needles and as it hits the water, it will form into an organic shape.

7. Turn off the torch, and place the crucible on the heat-resistant work surface.

8. Take the can to a sink and run cold water over it. Remove and separate the pine needles to find the silver. There may be more than one casting, so look carefully **(k, l)**.

9. Rinse, pickle, and brass brush.

10. Set the stone into the bezel using a #1 tip on the torch and following the basic procedure for soldering a bezel **(m)**. If your stone does not fit properly in the bezel cup, simply reapply the flame, lift the bezel and start the soldering procedure over.

11. Put easy solder on the back of the pine straw casting and position it on the pendant **(n)**. Using a medium flame, begin heating the casting and circling around the pendant. Remember to heat the big parts first, and in this case,

1. Make a pine straw bundle that completely fills a soup can and bind it with a rubber band **(a)**. Trim the tops of the pine needles flat and even with the top of the can **(b)**. Fill the can with water **(c)**.

2. The amount of silver you put in the crucible depends on your desired pendant size. For this pendant, I used ⅓ troy oz. Small thin pieces of scrap melt the quickest, so snip any larger pieces into smaller pieces **(d)**.

3. Place a small container of casting flux on the work surface. (I use a film canister with holes punched in the lid.) Put the metal can with the water and pine needles on the heat-resistant work surface. I prefer to set my can in my annealing pan **(e)**. Holding the crucible in your dominant hand and the torch in your non-dominant hand, begin heating the scrap **(f)**.

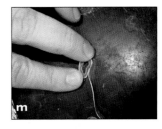

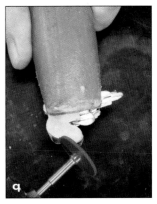

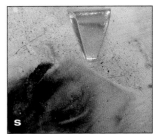

that is the casting. You don't want to melt the bezel **(o)**.

12. Pickle, rinse, and brass brush.

13. Use a jeweler's saw to remove all excess silver sheet from around the pendant **(p)**, and a flex shaft to smooth the sharp edges **(q)**.

14. Measure and cut a bail out of 24-gauge sterling sheet using the template on page 96 **(r)**.

15. Use looping pliers to bend the bail in half **(s)**.

16. Place a 2 mm ball of easy solder paste on the two touching ends, and

Season the crucible:

Your crucible must be seasoned before you use it so that the melted silver will flow out smoothly. To season a crucible you'll need to use a large bushy flame to preheat the crucible **(a)**. Put a small amount of casting flux in the crucible and heat again **(b, c)**. Continue adding flux and swirling it around in the crucible as it melts, coating the inside and spouts of your crucible with a glass-like layer **(d)**. Cool. You may need to repeat this a few times to completely coat your crucible.

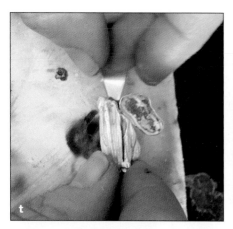

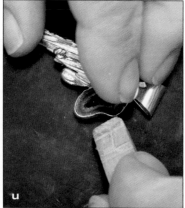

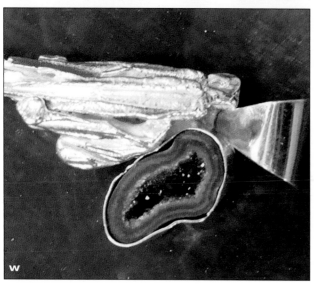

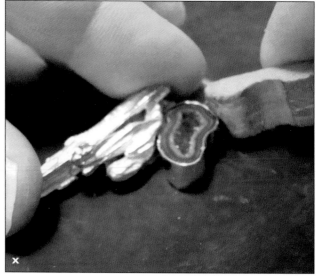

Bail Template (24-gauge metal)

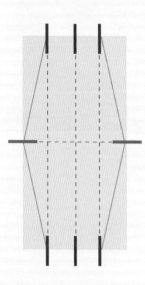

step 1
Divide width in half and mark on top and bottom.
step2
Divide each half in half again and mark.
step 3
Divide the length in half and mark.
step 4
Connect the points from step 2 with the points from step 3. Cut out with shears and fold over roundnose pliers.

solder the bail to the pendant **(t)**.

17. Pickle, rinse, and brass brush.

18. Shine or add patina to the pendant. The choice is yours. I put my piece in the tumbler overnight for a nice shine.

19. Position the stone in the bezel **(u)**. Use a clothespin half to begin folding down the edges of the bezel **(v)**. Continue until the entire bezel is folded over your stone **(w, x)**.

20. Use a burnisher to smooth out the edges **(y)**.

Chapter 4

Well now you've done it! You're running with the big dogs now! Hopefully by this time you've done most (if not all) of the other projects in the book and you are ready to tackle some more complicated projects. Each of these projects is based on skills you've built along the way—you're just applying more of them to each project.

Don't become discouraged with mistakes or setbacks. Some of my best pieces of work are the results of mistakes or plans gone bad. Look at all bumps in your designing world as artistic moments. Don't discard them: Just back up and punt. Try a new strategy. I want you to see that everyone, no matter who they are, or how accomplished they are, messes up sometimes. Metal melts, stones break, tools malfunction, and the best drawn-out design idea sometimes just does not work.

Robert Dancik once said, "If you get to a point in your piece where you look down and say, d#$n that looks good, stop there! You can never go back to that point if you continue. Stop there, and start another piece to attempt your original idea. You'll regret it if you don't." I think that one statement was worth the entire price of the workshop. We all see our work at a point when it is really something, but when we fuss beyond that point more often than not, we end up much less satisfied with the end result. I call this the "futz factor." Don't over-futz your work.

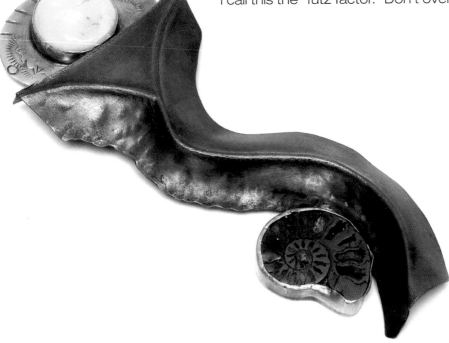

Nautilus Pendant

I first saw foldforming at a studio in Asheville, North Carolina, called Earthspeaks Studios, owned by Bill Churlick. One weekend Bill and I co-taught a class in which he taught foldforming on Saturday and I taught how to make something out of the forms using cold connections on Sunday. Of course, I participated in the foldforming portion of the workshop. Bill challenged us to continue hammering until we could make the metal loop all the way around. I did it, I did it! Now you can.

foldforming • liver of sulfur patina

Tool Kits
- Foldforming
- Annealing
- Wirewrapping

Tools
- Metal shears
- Bordering hammer
- Spring-loaded punch
- Hole punch, flexshaft, or drill and bit for a ¹⁄₁₆-in. hole
- Scribe or awl

Materials
- 1½ x 3-in. piece of 24-gauge copper sheet
- 1 ft. 18-gauge copper wire (depending on the embellishments used)
- Bead (or river rocks) for embellishment

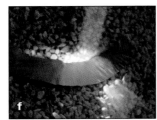

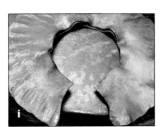

1. Cut a 1 ½ x 3-in. piece of copper.

2. Anneal the metal before you begin **(a)**. Fold the piece in half lengthwise **(b)**. (Note: The foldform for this piece is similar to the pod on page 27, but the corners of the metal are not cut.)

3. Place the folded piece of metal on the anvil and starting in the middle, use a bordering hammer to begin striking the folded edge in close power blows working down to the end **(c, d)**. Flip the metal over and begin again from the middle and strike down from the center to the other end **(e)**.

4. Anneal, quench, dry, and repeat **(f)**. (Don't pickle until it is finally unfolded.)

5. Continue to hammer, anneal, and repeat. Each time you repeat the hammering process, you

should see the metal piece take on more of a spiral shape. This should take approximately four times to complete **(g)**.

6. When the two ends are within ½ in. of each other, anneal the piece for a final time **(h)**. Rinse and dry.

7. Dimple locations in the top center of the spiral 1 in. apart. Drill two ¹⁄₁₆-in. holes, going through both sides of the metal **(i, j)**.

8. Carefully open the fold-form using an oyster knife or dull table knife. As you open, the two ends should begin to overlap **(k)**.

9. Shape with your hands as desired. If the overlap is too much, trim with shears.

10. Pickle, rinse, and brass brush.

11. Use liver of sulfur patina on the spiral and a length of 18-gauge copper wire.

12. Use a scribe or an awl to make a hole in the center of the back side of the spiral, just big enough to fit a piece of 18-gauge wire **(l)**. Wire-wrap the focal bead or beads on the piece of patinated 18-gauge wire. (This technique may vary, depending on your choice of stones).

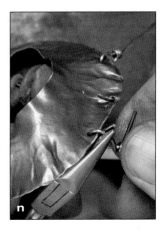

13. Thread the beaded wire up through the center of the spiral and fold the edge over. Hide the end in one of the hammered creases of the spiral and cut off the excess wire **(m)**.

14. Thread a piece of 18-gauge wire through each of the two side holes and make basic wire wraps to form loops to later attach chain **(n)**.

Open Wire Bezel Pendant

I originally designed this pendant to showcase another stone, one I got in Lake Lure, North Carolina. It was a crystalline structure with beautiful amber tones. As I was closing one of the prongs over it, it cracked down the middle. My heart sank into my stomach. I went for my stash and started looking through my seashells. I had a great looking piece of coral that we found in Pompano Beach, Florida. It fit in the prongs but was a little bit smaller than the original stone. Then, I pulled down my stones and premade bezel cups. Not only did the combination work, but I actually like the outcome better than the original design. Thank goodness for "artistic moments."

TIP If the bezel cup is too deep for the stone, you have several options. You can build up the bottom of the cup with cutouts from a credit card or gift card, make a ring of small wire, or use a tiny piece of polymer clay. Always use the dental floss under the stone when you put the stone in the cup so you will be able to remove the stone. If the stone fits in the cup at the right height, put the stone in the cup without the dental floss.

soldering • forming • liver of sulfur patina • setting a stone in a bezel cup

Tool Kits
- Soldering (paste)
- Patina

Tools
- Half a clothespin or burnisher
- Annealing pan
- File
- Roundnose or looping pliers
- Flex shaft with brown Cratex wheel

- Third hand
- Wire cutters
- Marker
- Pencil and paper

Materials
- 40–50 mm focal stone
- 7–11 mm round cabochon
- 1 ft. 11-gauge sterling silver wire, depending on focal stone

- 5 in. low-dome sterling silver wire, depending on the size and number of prongs
- **2** 10 mm vintage African brass rings (or any large jump rings)
- dental floss
- pre-made sterling silver bezel cup to fit cabochon

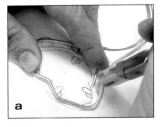

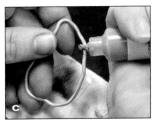
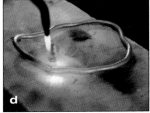

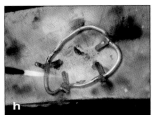

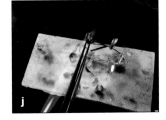

1. Trace the large stone on paper. Bend the 11-gauge wire to match the outline and form the bezel **(a)**.

2. Align the ends of the wire. File the ends flush **(b)**. Solder the wire bezel with hard solder paste **(c, d)**. Pickle, rinse, and brass brush.

3. Lay the bezel flat and place the stone inside. Measure the distance from the outside rim of the bezel wire to ⅛ in. beyond the edge of the stone. Multiply by two for the prong length **(e)**.

4. Cut four or more prongs to this length from the low-dome sterling wire. Round the edges of both ends of each wire with a file.

5. Use roundnose pliers to bend each prong in half **(f)**.

6. Mark spots on the bezel wire for the prongs and the two rings **(g)**. Position the

prongs and apply a 2 mm ball of medium solder paste inside the bend of each.

7. Solder all the prongs in one soldering operation **(h)**. Move the flame around the entire bezel, warming up the bezel and the prongs. Then move the flame directly around one prong. After the solder flows, move to the next prong. Continue until all the prongs are soldered in place. Pickle and rinse.

8. Stand the bezel upright using binding wire furniture (see page 36). Re-mark the ring locations if the marks disappeared in Step 7.

9. Hold a ring with cross-locking tweezers. Apply a 2 mm ball of easy solder paste.

10. Heat the bezel. Then, aim the flame at the attachment spot on the bezel for the first ring. Bring the ring down to

the bezel and hold it on the hot spot while continuing to apply heat **(i)**. When the solder flows, remove the flame, but hold the tweezers steady on the ring until the solder hardens. Pickle and rinse.

11. Take a deep breath and repeat with the second ring. Keep the flame as far away from the first ring as possible **(j)**. If the first ring falls off (it happens sometimes!), resolder with extra-easy solder paste. Pickle, rinse, and brass brush.

12. Use a flex shaft with a Cratex wheel to remove any unwanted solder.

13. Place a 2 mm ball of extra-easy solder paste on the back of the pre-made bezel cup. Place the cup on the wire bezel, begin heating the wire bezel, and quickly move the heat to the bezel cup. Don't overheat; watch for the solder to flow **(k)**.

14. Tumble the pendant or clean with a brass brush. Add patina, if you'd like.

15. Use a clothespin bezel pusher to push the edges of the cup over the stone **(l)**.

16. On a soft surface, position the stone in the bezel **(m)**. Begin closing the prongs around the stone. Push the prongs partially toward the stone on the front. Flip the piece and push the prongs partially on the back. Continue to gently push the prongs from the front and the back until the stone doesn't move in the setting. Moving the prongs in stages helps position the stone in the middle of the bezel.

Madonna Pendant

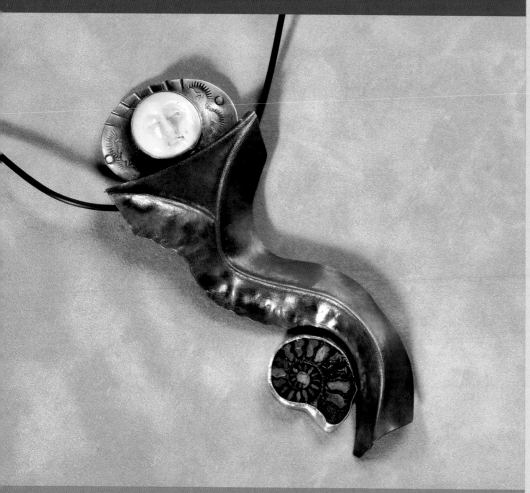

I made my first score fold at the Earthspeaks Studio. I carried it around for two years, not really knowing what to do with it. Finally one day I was staring at it once again, and I got to thinking it looked kind of like a mermaid. At the Gem and Lapidary Wholesale Show in Franklin, North Carolina, I found a booth with carved fossil ivory. **I started placing carved faces against the score fold until I found one that spoke to me.** A graceful face paired with a Blue London Topaz makes me think of the classic mother and child image. The rounder face in this project is matched with a fossil ammonite stone.

foldforming • score fold • silver soldering • bezels • texturing metals

Tool Kits
- Soldering
- Texturing

Tools
- Burnisher
- Rolling mill (optional) or heavy hammer and anvil
- Dental floss
- Marker

Materials
- Carved face cabochon
- Semiprecious gemstone cabochon
- 3 x 6-in. piece of 24-gauge copper sheet
- 26- or 24-gauge sterling silver sheet
- 3 in. 16-gauge sterling silver wire
- 6 in. fine silver bezel wire
- Silver solder paste: medium, easy, extra easy
- Medium sterling silver solder wire
- Steel binding wire
- Packing tape
- Polymer clay (optional)

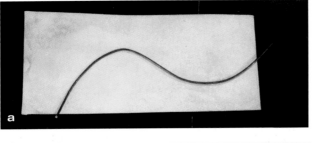

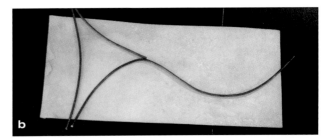

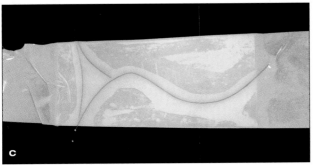

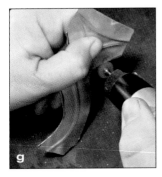

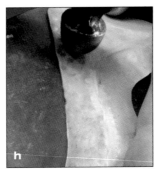

1. Anneal a 3 x 5-in. piece of 24-gauge copper sheet.

2. Make a sensuous S shape out of 20-gauge steel binding wire **(a)**, add two more pieces of wire to the top of the S to create a triangle **(b)**, and tape it to the back of the copper sheet with packing tape **(c)**. Cut the tape to the same width as the copper sheet, or the impression of the tape will show.

3. Using a heavy hammer on an anvil or a rolling mill, make a scored line in the copper sheet.

TIP If you are using a rolling mill, encase the metals in protective sheeting so the binding wire doesn't mar the rollers (d, e).

4. Remove the packing tape and the binding wire. Anneal the copper again. Pickle, rinse, and brass brush.

5. Mark an outline of the scored line ½ in. to ¾ in. from center on both sides. Saw along the outside of the lines **(f)**. File and smooth all rough edges **(g)**.

6. Use a hammer to texture on one side of the scored line **(h)**.

7. With your fingers, gently press the edges in toward the scored line **(i)**. Gently bend the metal with your fingers, starting at one end. Proceed up the sheet, working on each bend in turn in gentle stages rather than trying to bend too much at once **(j)**.

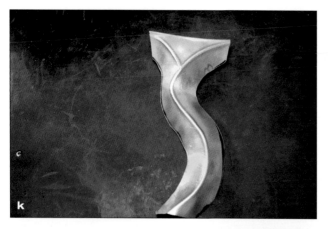

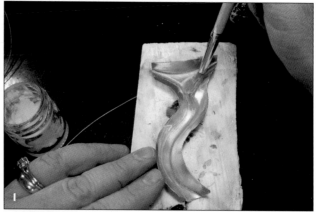

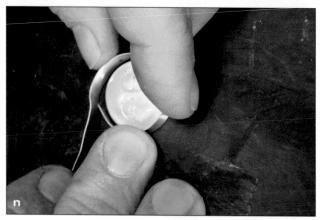

8. When you are pleased with the shape you have formed, reinforce the scored line with solder **(k)**. Apply flux along the inside groove of the scored line **(l)**. Place medium wire solder along the scored grove **(m)**. Apply heat until solder flows the entire length of the scored line. Pickle, rinse, and brass brush.

9. Measure around the outside diameter of the ivory face with bezel wire and snip off with metal shears where the ends meet **(n)**.

10. Align the ends of the bezel wire, place a 3 mm ball of hard solder paste on the touching ends of the bezel wire, and place it on the soldering board. Apply hard solder paste to the seam **(o)**. Gently heat the entire bezel

wire with a torch, moving in slow circles. Focus the flame on the solder, yet continue to move the flame gently so that the silver does not melt. When the flux built into the solder paste flames up, begin watching for the solder to flow. Once the solder begins to flow, remove the heat and let the bezel cool for a few seconds. Flip the bezel over and gently heat the other side of the bezel, drawing the solder all the way down the bezel wire.

11. Let the bezel cool a few more seconds. Pickle, rinse, and dry.

12. File away any excess solder.

13. Reposition the ivory face in the bezel so that the correct shape is recreated.

14. Cut a disk from the sterling silver sheet ½ in. larger in diameter than the bezel. Place the bezel on the disk.

15. Eye the position you desire by placing the copper component and the bezel on the round disk and mark it **(p)**.

16. Remove the ivory face, and place 2 mm balls of medium solder paste around the inside bottom rim of the bezel wire, spacing solder about ⅛ in. apart **(q)**. Place the bezel back down in the spot you marked. Using the torch, gently begin heating up the outside portion of the sterling silver disk, slowly circling in to the bezel wire. Continue to heat in a circular pattern, but begin to focus some of the

heat on the inside of the bezel. As the flux in the paste begins to flare up, do not remove the heat, but continue to gently move the torch, focusing the heat inside the bezel **(r)**. You should see the solder flow about 30 seconds after the flux flares up. Gently pull the flame outside of the bezel and move it so the solder flows all the way around the bezel. (You may need to gently push down the bezel wire with tweezers.) Cool for a few seconds, pickle, and rinse.

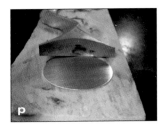

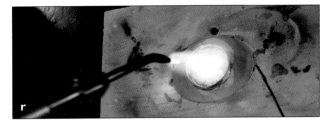

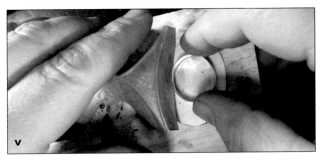

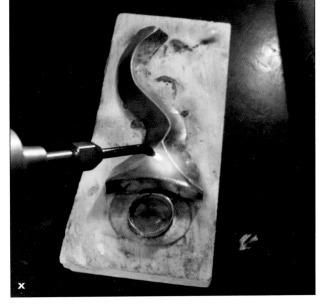

17. File away any extra silver solder.

18. Repeat Steps 9–14 and 16–17 to set the semi-precious stone **(s)**.

19. Use a jeweler's saw to saw away excess silver around the stone component **(t)**. File edges flush against the bezel wire **(u, v)**.

20. Arrange the copper component on the large silver disk and mark its placement.

21. Place five or six 2 mm balls of easy solder paste on the underside of the copper component where the silver disk will be attached **(w)**.

22. Place the copper component on top of the silver disk in the spot you marked in Step 20. Using the torch, gently begin heating the copper component. Move the flame in gentle lazy circles ,moving across the silver as well **(x)**. (Try to keep your flame as far away from the bezel wire as possible.)

When the flux flares up, begin watching for the solder to flow. Angle the flame down under the copper component once you see a sign of the solder flowing on top **(y)**.

23. Remove the flame and let the piece cool for a few seconds. Pickle, rinse, dry, and file away extra solder.

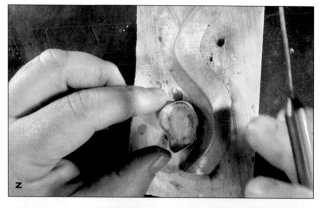

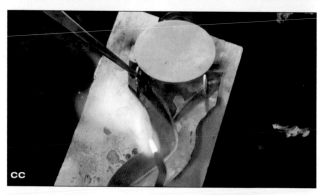

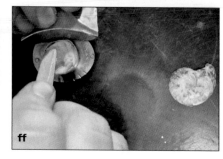

24. Repeat Steps 20–23 for the stone bezel **(z)**.

25. Using the medium barrel of medium stepped pliers, make two 16-gauge sterling silver jump rings.

26. Hold a jump ring in cross-locking tweezers and place a 2 mm ball of extra-easy solder at the join. Begin applying heat to the copper component at what would be the "shoulder" of the pendant **(aa)**. Place the jump ring on the heated portion while continuing to heat **(bb)**. Hold the jump ring steady as the solder flows. When the

solder has flowed, hold the jump ring steady for a few seconds after removing the flame. Pickle and rinse.

(Note: Make binding wire furniture to support the bezel at the top of the pendant. Leaving this portion suspended in the air while soldering the jump rings on the back might allow the sterling bezel to heat up and come off of the copper.)

27. Solder the second jump ring on the opposite side of the pendant in the same way **(cc)**. Pickle, rinse, and brass brush.

28. Remove excess solder with a flex shaft and Cratex wheel.

29. Using a straight-edge stamp, texture around the bezel of the top component **(dd)**.

30. Place the whole piece in a liver of sulfur solution until desired patina is achieved. Remove, rinse, dry, and sand away enough of the liver of sulfur using 0000 steel wool to reveal the texture **(ee)**.

31. Set the ivory face and the stone in the bezels using a burnisher or a half a clothes-

pin. Picturing a compass, apply pressure first at the north and south sides, and then at the east and west sides **(ff)**. Continue moving the burnisher around the stones until the entire bezel is pushed over the girdle and they do not wiggle inside. (Some bezels may have to be trimmed to accommodate the faces and stones before they are soldered down in Step 16, or layers of padding may need to be added underneath to raise the stones so they don't sit too low in the bezel cup.)

Antler Pendant

Believe it or not, deer antlers are not hard to come by. I am not a hunting enthusiast, but I was in a taxidermy shop looking for glass eyeballs (another story completely) when I saw some deer antlers on the work table. I was drawn to the beautiful texture and colors of the antlers. I asked the proprietor about them, and he said he had loads of them and offered me some. Well, antlers in hand, I was one happy camper. Since then I have had many opportunities to obtain more. Just ask around. They're out there! Many hunters throw them away after they process the meat. I recently discovered that deer shed their antlers each year and grow them back, so you may be able to get your hands on some antlers without the deer having to meet its demise first. What a great way to recycle something beautiful.

soldering • riveting

Tool Kits
- Soldering
- Patina
- Wirewrapping
- Cold connections
- Sawing

Tools
- Third hand
- Face mask
- Flex shaft with brown Cratex wheel and mizzy wheel
- Half clothespin or bezel pusher
- Drill with 1.25 mm drill bit
- Dental floss

Materials
- Antler section
- 24-gauge sterling silver sheet
- Fine bezel wire
- 4 mm half round wire
- 18-gauge sterling silver wire
- 4 mm flat wire
- 10 x 15 mm tube-shaped sterling silver bead
- 8–10 mm cabochon
- Two-part epoxy

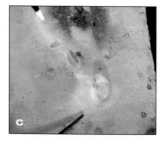

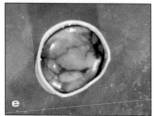

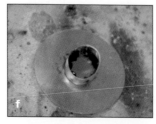

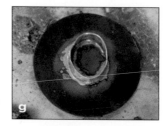

1. Use a jeweler's saw (or a hacksaw if you have one) and cut off a section of the antler **(a)**. Note: Wear a face mask or work under a dust collector. Sawing bone smells horrible and the dust can't be good for you.

2. Use sandpaper or a flex shaft with a mizzy wheel to grind and smooth the antler down to a pleasing shape. (A mizzy wheel is a compressed abrasive wheel that is like a little grindstone.)

3. Wrap a piece of fine bezel wire around the stone and cut to size **(b)**. Solder bezel closed with hard solder **(c)**.

4. File away extra solder with the flex shaft and brown Cratex wheel **(d)**.

5. Place the stone back in the bezel wire to verify a good fit and shape **(e)**. Remove the stone.

6. Solder the bezel to a piece of 24-gauge sheet with medium solder **(f, g)**. Pickle, rinse, and brass brush.

7. Stretch a piece of dental floss across the bezel and trial-set the stone. Remove the stone.

8. Use a flex shaft with a brown Cratex wheel to clean any excess solder.

9. Cut the leftover silver sheet around the bezel to a shape that complements the piece of antler and file the edges smooth. Leave a straight edge across the top of the sheet so it can be soldered to the bar across the top of the antler **(h)**.

10. Cut a piece of 4 mm flat wire to form a bar across the top of the antler. The piece may be as long as or shorter than the width of the antler **(i)**.

11. Secure a separate, ¼-in. piece of 4 mm flat wire in the tweezers of a third hand. Place a 2 mm ball of hard solder paste on the bottom tip of the wire. Position the third hand so the wire is resting in the center of the 4 mm flat wire bar on the solder board **(j)**. Solder the two pieces together. Begin heating the wire section on the solder board, slowly moving in toward the wire being held by the third hand. Watch for the solder to flow **(k)**. Pickle, rinse, and dry.

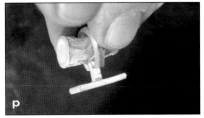

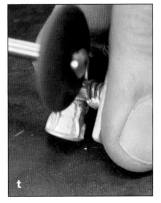

12. Hold a sterling silver tube or tube-shaped bead with a third hand **(l)**. Cut the post to a height appropriate to your pendant (the one in this project is about ¼-in. high) and file it flat across the top. Place a 2 mm ball of medium solder paste on the top of the post. Position the tube being held by the third hand so that it rests on top of the post **(m)**. Begin heating up the tube, then move the flame to the base. Gently move the heat to the solder join **(n)**. Pickle, rinse, and dry.

13. Cut a piece of half-round wire to fit over the tube **(o, p)**.

14. Place a small amount of extra-easy solder between the half-round wire and the tube and solder **(q)**. Solder together with medium flame **(r)**. Pickle, rinse, and brass brush.

15. Wrap a piece of 18-gauge wire around the remaining post section beneath the half-round wire as a decoration **(s)**. (It will be soldered later.)

16. File the end of the half-round wire so it slopes down to the post **(t, u)**.

17. The antler will be riveted to the back unit through the flat bar going across the antler. Dimple a spot in the long flat bar with a spring-loaded punch, then drill a ¹⁄₁₆-in. hole on one side of the post. Repeat on the other side of the post. The rivets connecting the bail and the antler go through these holes.

TIP Put a piece of wood under the metal—I used a chop stick between the tube and the base.

18. Position the bail on top of the antler and mark the top of the antler through the hole in the bail.

19. Drill two holes about 1 mm in diameter in the top of the antler where marked. **(v–y)**.

20. Attach the setting and bezel for the stone to the bail unit using extra-easy solder. The straight portion of the sheet should butt up against the flat wire. Solder the 18-gauge wire coiled around the post in Step 15 in this step as well **(z)**.

v

w

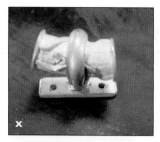

x

y

z

aa

bb

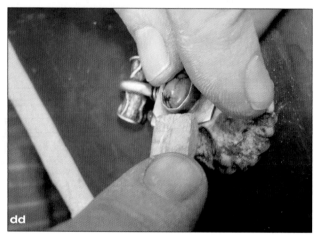

dd

cc

ee

21. Cut two 1-in. pieces of 18-gauge sterling wire and draw a bead on the end of each wire. Flatten the beads of the wires to create a nail-head rivet.

22. Cut the wire and thread it through the holes drilled in Step 19 **(aa)**.

23. Bend the rivet wires so you can guide them into the holes in the antler **(bb)**.

24. Place all the silver pieces (bail unit and rivets) in a warm liver of sulfur solution. Rinse and dry.

25. Mix some two-part epoxy and place a dab on each wire rivet, and place and secure in the antler **(cc)**.

26. Dab some mixed two-part epoxy underneath the bezel where it is covering the flat of the antler.

27. Gently tap the edges of the pendant flush against the antler with a soft blow hammer.

28. Use a bezel pusher as necessary to set the stone in the pendant **(dd, ee)**.

Final Words

There is no way I can thank all the people who have made it possible for me to write this book. I have to start with the most obvious, my family. Thanks to my husband, Norm, and my daughter, Nora. They put up with my frustrations with the computer and came to my rescue more than once. They both have virtually no interest in metalsmithing, but now know more than they ever wanted to know about it!. Nora, with the help of Steve Webb, did an outstanding job of converting pictures and labeling them correctly. My son, Chase, who was six when I wrote this book, was very patient with me and the amount of time it took me to write. He only once said, "I don't care about your dumb book!" Because of the age difference between our children, there has never been sibling rivalry, but the writing of this book took on a life of its own and became the closest he'll ever have to a rival for my time. Norm—anyone who knows me knows that Norm and I are a package deal. If there's Kim, then there's Norm, and vice-versa. There's no separation between us, so this is his book as much as it is mine. There would be no book without Norm.

Mixed Metal Mania became possible because of the wonderful students I have had over the years. The projects, tips, and techniques all evolved from answering student's questions, or by working through design element issues presented by students. I owe all that I am as an instructor and metalsmith to my students. They keep me motivated and inspired. Thank you everyone! I love you, and hope to continue this relationship!

I have to thank Margaret Bray. She has become, I can safely say, my closest friend. She became photographer, go-fer, and sounding board. She's there when I need her, and never expects anything in return. I depend on her immensely. She tells everyone she works for food, but I could never repay her for her time and friendship. We both learned a lot about book writing and about each other. Thank you, Margaret, and your family, for putting so much time and effort into making this book possible.

I would also like to thank Karen Jensen. One of my most loyal students, she now is one of my best friends! Our relationship has evolved to the point where there is little distinction between student and teacher. We both share all of our knowledge with each other freely.

Dan Haga, my mentor and friend. Without his tutelage and technical advice, I wouldn't be as skilled a silversmith as I am. I have only just scratched the surface of the knowledge he has to share and hope to keep learning from him so that his legacy in the jewelry industry will continue on.

Last and most obviously, I want to thank my parents. They are always there for me, and have always supported me in whatever I have tried to do—sometimes with trepidation, but they let me experiment anyway. They were behind me when I left my comfortable and secure teaching career to pursue my artistic dream. When I called my mom to tell her my plan, she replied, "I'll go to any show, anywhere, if you'll put your notice in tomorrow and not be talked out of it." She believed in me! My dad is my strength. I depend on his advice and approval for everything.

If you read all the way through the acknowledgments, then I thank you too! You must be one of my family, friends or students. If not, then now you are! Thank you!

Here's Where You Can Find Me:

St. Jean Studio of Jewelry Arts
kimstjean.com

William Holland School of Lapidary Arts
lapidaryschool.org

John C. Campbell Folk School
folkschool.org

Bead&Button Show
beadandbuttonshow.com

Beadfest and Beadfest Wire
www.beadfest.com

Women Creative
barbaramcguire.com

My Garden of Beadin'
mygardenofbeadin.com

Tryon Arts and Crafts Council
tryonartsandcrafts.org

CREATE YOUR STYLE with SWAROVSKI ELEMENTS Tucson Events
create-your-style.com

Everything you wanted ... and MORE!

30 MOR PROJECT FROM KIM ST. JE

You loved this book of projects and didn't want it to end, right?

HOW TO
Etch, Pierce,
Enamel,
and Set
Striking Jewelry

Kim St. Jean

64933 • $21.95

Well, guess what — there's more!

Continue your love affair with Kim St. Jean's amazing metalwork in her next book, *Metal Magic*.

You'll discover essential tips and tricks for taking basic metalworking to the next level. In addition to the must-have 35-page guide to techniques, you'll enjoy 30 projects that teach you how to

- build color with enameling
- add detail with etching
- create unique settings
- and more!

dictator ruler with no restrictions on their power, such as the possibility of being voted out of power. Hitler and Stalin were both dictators

double agent secret agent who is actually working for the organization or country they are supposed to be spying on

Holocaust the organised murder of millions of Jews and other people by the Nazis during World War II

incendiary type of bomb designed to start a fire

intelligence information gathered during wartime, often using secret agents or other hidden means

minefield area covered with hidden explosive devices called mines

misinformation information that is deliberately designed to mislead the enemy

neutral not involved in a war, and not favouring one side or the other

persecute singling out a person or group for harsh or unfair treatment

propaganda information designed to present a particular view, usually that of the government

puppet government government without much real power that has to follow the orders of another power, such as the government set up in southern France during World War II

sabotage deliberate damage to transport or other enemy facilities designed to disrupt military or political forces, such as blowing up railway lines

Soviet Union country made up of what are now Russia, Ukraine and several other countries. The Soviet Union broke up in 1991

FIND OUT MORE

Books

See Inside the Second World War by Rob Lloyd Jones and Maria Cristina Pritelli (Usborne, 2011)

Eyewitness: World War II (DK, 2014 edition)

True Stories of the Second World War by Paul Dowswell (Usborne, 2014)

History Relived: The Home Front by Cath Senker and Camilla Lloyd (Wayland, 2012)

Real Lives: Winston Churchill by Harriet Castor (A & C Black, 2012)

The Diary of a Young Girl by Anne Frank is an essential book for anyone who wants to understand what it was like to grow up hiding from the Nazis in occupied Europe.

There are many other fiction books about World War II that can give you an idea of what it was like to live through the events described in this book.

Online resources

The National Archives have created a fantastic online resource covering many aspects of World War II

http://www.nationalarchives.gov.uk/education/worldwar2/

The Imperial War Museum is home to a vast collection of artefacts and resources from the war. It's well worth a visit but you can also discover lots through the museum's website at **www.iwm.org.uk**

There are many other museums that tell the story of the war. Your local museum may explain how your home town was changed by the war. Other museums tell the story of certain aspects of the conflict, such as the National Army Museum. Find out more at **www.nam.ac.uk**

You can also find out more about other countries and how they remember the war. The Australian National War memorial website is a great place to find out about Australians' experiences in World War II **www.awm.gov.au/atwar/ww2/**

The United States Holocaust Memorial Museum includes lots of resources and information about the wartime persecution of Jews and others **www.ushmm.org**

A The National Archives

The National Archives is home to more than 1,000 years of the nation's history. From Shakespeare's will and Domesday Book to beautiful designs and photographs, its unique historical collection is one of the largest in the world. We hold an extensive collection of records covering the history of the Second World War, including operational records, military maps, recommendations for gallantry awards, prisoners of war records, minutes from cabinet meetings, the 1939 Register and records concerning the production of food and military materials.

www.nationalarchives.gov.uk

The National Archives picture acknowledgements and catalogue references

P5 DEFE 2/40 (2) D-Day War Diary 4 Commando 6 June 1944. P5 DEFE 2/499 D-Day, Mulberry B, looking SW 1944. P6 FO 96/221 No55 Handshakes for the Fuehrer at the Nazi Party Rally, Nuremberg 1933. P6 No53 Marching the flags at the Nazi Party Rally, Nuremberg 1933. P8 PREM 1/331A Telegram to Winston Churchill concerning Hitler's invasion of Poland, 1939. P9 PREM 1/266A The Munich agreement intelligence paper 30 September 1938. P9 FO 898/527 German troops occupy Poland 1939. P10 FO 898/527 French and British evacuees from Dunkirk 1943-19. P10 INF 3/1578 Air duel over crowded evacuation beach, Dunkirk Artist Bryan de Grineau 1939-1946. P11 INF 3/1436 (A) Hitler, with bloody sword, standing on France and contemplating invasion of England 1939-1946. P12 INF 1/244 Winston Churchill 1944-1944. P13 AIR 22/262 no 14387 RAF casualties 15 August 1940. P13 INF 1/244 Battle of Britain pilots and air gunners, possibly from a Defiant Squadron 1944-1944. P13 INF 1/264 Public morale, daily report 23 August 1940. P14 AIR 2/5238 Bombing of Coventry 1940. RDF stations 1940. P15 HO 193/1 Bomb Census map, East London 7-14 October 1940. P15 INF 2/44 London after the Blitz, St Paul's Cathedral 1944-1945. P15 FO 898/527 St Paul's Cathedral, London, obscured by smoke of bombs during the Blitz 1940. P16 KV 2/462 Edward Chapman (Zigzag) Chapman's ID card created by Nazi forgers 1941. P16 KV 2/862 Johann Jebsen anti-Nazi intelligence officer, British double agent code name Artist during the Second World War. P17 WO 208/4374 Juan Pujol-Garcia (codename Garbo) The Garbo network (written) World War II 1949-1949. P18 HW 25/3 Mathematical theory of ENIGMA machine by Alan Turing. P19 FO 850/234 Colossus electronic digital computer 1943. P21 EXT 1/48 Comrades in Arms (Churchill and Stalin) 1939-1945. P22 INF 13/213 World War II poster - The War Against Japan 1939-1945. P23 INF 3/791T Ditty Box Hitler boxer and Franklin Roosevelt Artist Wyndham Robinson 1939-1946. P24 INF 3/80 General Sir Bernard Montgomery 1939-1946. P24 PREM 3/109 Churchill to Wavell regarding the defence of Crete 28 April 1941. P25 WO 201/2846 Western Desert deception, dummy 25pdr gun made at Tobruk 1942. P25 DEFE 2/609 Operation Torch North Africa November 1942. P25 INF 3/1265 Grand Harbour, Malta, under air attack Artist Rowland Hilder 1939-1946. P26 KV 4/284 German sabotage chocolate bar 1942-1943. P27 MF 1/27 Locations of resistance groups and saboteurs in Northern Italy 1943-1945. P27 INF 2/7 French World War II poster - Salut A La Resistance 1945-1945. P28 HS 6/597 French resistance, arms deliveries by region 1942. P28 HS 7/49 Explosive rat 1941-1945. P29 HS 8/1032 SOE fake passport for Hitler p2 1941-1945. P29 HS 7/28 Incendiary Suitcase 1944. P30 ADM 205/30 New U-Boat bunker with bomb-proof roof at St Nazaire 9 December 1942. P31 MFQ 1/588 Allied merchant ships sunk in the Battle of The Atlantic, September 1939. P31 AIR 27/1568 U-570, first U-Boat captured by the British in WWII, surrenders to HMS Kingston Agate. P32 BT 131/40 Rationing Adult's Ration Book. P32 INF 3/225 Make do and mend Stuffed doll figure patching cloth 1939-1946. P33 MAF 102/15 War Cookery Calendar, May-June 1943-1952. P33 INF 13/140 World War II poster - Dig For Victory 1939-1945. P34 RAIL 1057/3280 Women war workers on railways 1939-1945. P35 INF 2/42 ATS girls plotting 1940-1943. P35 INF 13/140 World War II poster - Lend A Hand On The Land - Join The Women's Land Army. P35 INF 3/403 Women for Industry Women of Britain. Come into the factories Artist Zec 1939-1946. P36 INF 3/86 Evacuation of children Artist Showell 1939-1946. P36 HO 294/612 Czechoslovak Refugee Trust case papers (Kindertransport) 1938-1956. P37 DO 131/15 CORB children to New Zealand 1940-1941. P37 INF 14/12 Children learning to 'Dig For Victory'. P38 INF 3/137 War Effort and they will say this was our finest hour Artist Pat Keely 1939-1946. P39 DEFE 1/332 Postal and Telegraph Censorship Department worker checks the content of a letter 1939-1945. P39 KV 2/346 William Joyce (Lord Haw Haw) 1940-1946. P39 INF 2/37 Publicity material distributed from Cairo 1943-1949. P41 INF 2/3 World War II poster - Together 1943-1943. P41 WO 106/5921 Operation Mincemeat (The Man Who Never Was), ID card 1943. P41 WO 106/5921/4 Operation Mincemeat correspondence 1943. P42 INF 2/4 Avro Lancaster 1943-1944. P42 INF 2/43 Air Chief Marshal Sir Arthur T Harris 1944. P42 AVIA 53/627 Mr Barnes Wallis plans for bouncing bomb Operation Chastise Dambusters. P43 AIR 16/487 Bomber Command, accuracy of bombing of German cities graph 11, Oct 1945. P43 AIR 16/487 Bomber Command, devastation of German cities graph 10A, Oct 1945. P44 WO 205/173 Operation Titanic, dummy parachutists diversionary plan D-Day, 1944. P44 HW 1/2784 Ultra decrypt noting German observation of Operation Overlord May 1944. P45 HO 338/27 Troops climb through bomb damage debris, Caen 1944. P46 CN 11/8 Polish Jews stacking clothing 1942. P48 FO 371/30917 Reports of German plan to exterminate Jews August 1942. P49 FO 371/42806 Sketch of Auschwitz concentration camp by a former prisoner 1944. P49 HW 16/6 Part1 Intercept about the Holocaust September 1942. P50 NSC 5/96 Wings for Victory the Sky's the limit 1943. P50 FO 898/527 A boy surveys ruins in Warsaw, Poland 1943-1945. P51 CAB 106/1010 Nazi prisoners in Aachen October 1944. P51 CAB 106/1080 Surrender of all forces under German control signed at Berlin 8 May 1945. P51 AIR 20/4376 100-person Public Surface shelter at East India Dock Road, London, after flying bomb strike 4 August 1944. P52 INF 14/447 Yalta conference Churchill Stalin Roosevelt 1945. P53 INF 3/391 Anti-Japanese Posters Smash Japanese aggression RAF raid on Japanese flying boats Artist Roy Nockolds 1939-1946. P54 PREM 3/66/7 Stalin's tick on Churchill's note written at the Kremlin on 9 October 1944, dividing up the Balkans into spheres of influence 9 October 1944. P55 WO 309/217 Confession by Rudolf Hoess, Kommandant of Auschwitz, to the killing of two million prisoners of war 16 March 1946. P56 INF 2/43 Red Cross worker writing letter for wounded soldier 1939-1945.

Index

Picture Acknowledgements

Front cover: All images Shutterstock aside from the following: INF 3/403 Women for Industry Women of Britain, Come into the factories 1939-1946, Artist Zec. INF 1/244 Battle of Britain pilots and air gunners, possibly from a Defiant Squadron 1944-1944. INF 2/1 pt2 (516) Winston Churchill by Cecil Beaton 1939-1945. EXT 1/57 (2) World War II poster - Dig For Victory. INF 3/1571 Tank crew surrendering to British infantry, Artist Marc Stone. Press Agency photographer/Wikimedia.

Back cover: All images Shutterstock aside from the following: FO 96/221 No55 Handshakes for the Fuehrer at the Nazi Party Rally, Nuremberg 1933. HO 193/1 Bomb Census map, East London 7-14 October 1940. INF 3/80 General Sir Bernard Montgomery 1939-1946. INF 3/137 And they will say this was our finest hour, Artist Pat Keely 1939-1946. Mark Higgins/Shutterstock.

Inside images all Shutterstock aside from the following: p4 top 92424169 Roger Viollet/Getty Images, p4 bottom 488661231 PhotoQuest/Getty Images, p6 middle Ralf Roletschek/Wikimedia, p7 82139236 Paul Popper/Popperfoto/Getty Images, p8 bottom Brian C. Weed/Shutterstock, p9 top Right_Honourable_Neville_Chamberlain._Wellcome_M0003096/Wellcome/Wikimedia, p11 U.S. National Archives and Records Administration /Wikimedia, p13 top Paul Drabot/Shutterstock, p14 top Peteri/Shutterstock, p15 top U.S. National Archives and Records Administration/Wikimedia, p17 top 3395126 Kurt Hutton/Picture Post/Getty Images, p17 top right The National Archives INF3/267/Wikimedia, p18 top Mark Higgins/Shutterstock, p18 middle 520714001 Fine Art Images/Heritage Images/Getty Images, p19 top Antoine Taveneaux/Wikimedia, p20 Johannes Hähle/Wikimedia, p21 Max Alpert/RIA Novosti archive/image #543/Alpert /CC-BY-SA 3.0/Wikimedia, p23 top 106501480 Keystone-France/Getty Images, p23 middle U.S. National Archives and Records Administration/Wikimedia, p23 bottom U.S. National Archives and Records Administration/Wikimedia, p26 3424802G201 Three Lions/Getty Images, p31 U.S. Navy/Wikimedia, p33 3318150 lava Katamidze Collection/Getty Images, p40 107759074 Galerie Bilderwelt/Getty Images, p43 118123779 Alinari Archives/Getty Images, p45 Archives Normandie 1939-45/Wikimedia, p46 170986804 Sovfoto/Getty Images, p47 500838679 Universal History Archive /Getty Images, p47 bottom Takkk/Wikimedia, p48 170980443 Sovfoto/Getty Images, p52 Hayakawa/Wikimedia, p53 top Charles Levy/Wikimedia, p53 middle US government photo/Wikimedia, p54 Robert Knudsen/Wikimedia, p55 United States Government/Wikimedia, p56 Bertl123/Shutterstock, p57 (top) Frankemann/Wikimedia, p57 (middle) Noppasin/Shutterstock, p57 (bottom) PlusONE/Shutterstock.